Table of Contents

Foreword

by David Sobel

Nature-based Early Childhood Education

As academic expectations in public elementary schools have become more demanding over the past decade, some educators have turned to the outdoors as a means of providing meaningful, relevant and tangible experiences for their students. The Forest Kindergarten movement, which took hold in Europe about 50 years ago, adopted a very different approach towards early childhood education. Instead of focusing on early literacy and numeracy skills, nature preschool and forest kindergarten educators aspired to developing social competence, individual resilience and a readiness to learn in young children. There are now 1,000 Forest Kindergartens in Germany, and 10% of the early childhood programs in Denmark are nature-based. The conviction of these educators is that this real natural world experience provides the confidence, resilience and perseverance that are the foundation for increased motivation and improved academic performance in students.

One form of this new approach in the United States is Forest Days, one day a week in the woods, year-round, in all kinds of weather, for public school children and teachers. Eliza Minnucci and Meg Teachout were two of the early initiators of this approach in a rural Vermont elementary school. Since then, dozens of teachers in Vermont, then in New Hampshire and around New England, and now across North America are implementing the same approach. Now there's fort-building, firewood-collecting, tree-climbing, belly-sliding, animal tracking, fox and geese playing in the woods behind the school on Forest Days. And literacy and math aren't thrown out the window. Instead, letter-making with sticks, acorn gathering and counting, following recipes, and doing science experiments all lead to the enhancement of the core curriculum. Children are learning their letters and numbers **and** getting stronger and healthier. It's a win-win situation.

Solving the Couch Potato Problem

Forest Days are one response to the academification, digitalization and indoorification of children's lives. Children spend eight hours a day interacting with screens and ½ hour a day outside. We're cultivating this screen habit by giving three year olds tablets, and this is concerning to parents. It's concerning because the lack of physical activity in children's lives and the disassociation between children and the natural world leads to unhealthy children and an un-cared-for natural world. Forest Days programs are reassuring and invigorating for both children and their parents. In a case study of these programs, one parent articulated some of the benefits:

"I was concerned about this program because my daughter had zero interest in nature when the school year was starting. But we're Vermonters so all we have is the outdoors, so to have a kid who didn't want to go outdoors was a bummer. But now she will look at us and she'll say, 'Let's go on a nature

Children are learning their letters and getting stronger and healthier.

"Students learn to collaborate as they spontaneously work together to build shelters, bridges or scale small rock walls and fallen trees."

– Cathy Newton
Principal
Ottauquechee
School, Vermont

walk!' And I'm thinking, 'What did you do with my child?' This happened within the first four Wednesdays! That has been awesome for our family because we thought we just had an 'indoor kid.'

"Before this she was into nail polish and 'What are you going to do for me?' and now she's out there building fairy houses and coming home with science skills and rocks in her pockets."

Something Old, Something New

For Vermonters in particular, this isn't a new idea, but the resurgence of an old idea. Take a typical Vermont childhood as described by Ida Clee Bemis born in East Calais, Vermont in 1878. In her recollections she describes a favorite spring activity.

"Another favorite pastime was mud cake making. We each had our mud cake house in the wood shed. We prepared regular meals using different kinds of leaves for beefsteak and pork chops. We frosted our cakes with sawdust. How we treasured the handle-less cups and pitchers and cracked plates we collected from all the neighbors!"

And in the winter,

"Our favorite sport was coasting. The skating season was short as it usually snowed as soon as the millpond froze over. We made the most of it while it lasted, the boys building a fire on the island so we could get warm. But coasting was something else again. We coasted from the day of the first snow until spring. Our favorite place was the road up the East Hill. We started almost up to the cemetery and coasted down to the church in the village, a good quarter of a mile."

These adventures in the landscape should be a Vermont child's birthright, something every child deserves to experience. They are activities that craft the unique hearty character of a Vermonter—the ability to live by your wits, the toughness to endure cold and hardship, the ingenuity to improvise and do more with less. Yet, in the past few decades fewer and fewer children have been experiencing this birthright. Programs like Forest Fridays revive these opportunities and insure the grittiness of future Vermonters.

And really, shouldn't all children, in all regions of the country, have these kinds of experiences in their everyday lives—swinging on vines in Illinois, wading in sandy streams and searching for shark teeth in Florida, making backyard bows and arrows in Arizona.

If you agree, then this handbook can be your trail guide. Starting a Forest Days program doesn't have to cost a lot of money. Many administrators will agree this is a good idea or they're convincible. And parents will thank you when their children come home with rosy cheeks. As Eliza says in The Best Day Ever documentary:

"Once you start getting out there, your trust in your children and your trust in nature as an environment for good learning will grow. And I think, before you know it, you'll be outside all day and not wanting to come back in and get on the bus."

Forest Day programs are reassuring and invigorating for both children and their parents.

A Forest Days Handbook

Program Design for School Days Outside

Written by Eliza Minnucci

with Meghan Teachout

Foreword by David Sobel

ANTIOCH UNIVERSITY

NEW ENGLAND

Green Writers Press
Brattleboro, Vermont

Published by Green Writers Press, Brattleboro, Vermont

Printed in the United States
10 9 8 7 6 5 4 3 2 1

Green Writers Press is a Vermont-based publisher whose mission is to spread a message of hope and renewal through the words and images we publish. We will adhere to our commitment to preserving and protecting the natural resources of the earth. To that end, a percentage of our proceeds will be donated to social-justice and environmental activist groups. Green Writers Press gratefully acknowledges the generosity of individual donors, friends, and readers to help support the environment and our publishing initiative. For information about funding or getting involved in our publishing program, contact Green Writers Press.

Giving Voice to Writers & Artists Who Will Make the World a Better Place
Green Writers Press | Brattleboro, Vermont
greenwriterspress.com
ISBN: 978-1-7322662-6-1

All photos by Eliza Minnucci except:
    Cover, page 21, 25, 38: Amanda Soule and Lauren Skilling
    Page 6 & 10: Amanda King
    Page 66: Christina Wild
    Page 67: Meghan Teachout
Book design and production: RavenMark, Inc.
Book printing: Villanti Printers
Illustrations: Kateryna; BloomUA; Linda Mirabile

Funding to support the writing, design and publication of the book came from the George B. Storer Foundation of Jackson, WY.

Acknowledgements

Amos Kornfeld
Thank you for being the first to say "Try it!" You led our school with an enthusiasm for passionate teaching and you were the foundation for our innovation.

David Sobel
Thank you for creating a home for nature-based educators, in your writing and at Antioch University New England. You are a door-opener, an amplifier and a champion.

Amy Butler
Thank you for so graciously sharing your poison ivy identification, Barred Owl call and your experience as a leader in outdoor-based public education.

Jack Hutchinson
Thank you for teaching us to build, not just shelters, but the confidence of our students, young and old. You make experts of us all.

Cabot Teachout and Keith Minnucci
Thank you for valuing our passions and wearing the babies when we go to work.

The Ottauquechee School Community
One does not take a whole class of five year olds out into the elements every week without a lot of help from the school secretary, custodians, cooks, nurse, special educators, paraprofessionals and cheerful teachers across the hall. Thank you for being a great home for a new teacher, a great home for a new idea, a great home for students.

Teachers
We have so much gratitude for all the teachers who have adopted the Forest Day idea and shaped it into your own wonderful thing. You inspire and energize, and give us hope in all the magical things that can, and do happen in schools.

"When I went into the forest I became a woodpecker then I was a kid again."
– Kindergartner Ottauquechee School, Vermont

Our Story

In 2013, Meg Teachout and I set out to take my public school kindergartners to the forest one day, every week throughout the school year. We hoped that the forest was a better place for five year olds to learn. We were motivated by the possibility of better academic and social outcomes for our students.

We went to the woods to be better teachers and students, to fill our days with more enthusiasm and authenticity. We went for muddy hands and sweaty brows, for running and shouting, for awed-gasps and belly laughs. We found them. We found challenges for each student and success for them all. We found great math lessons, new vocabulary and student driven science. We found independence, responsibility and pride. The endeavor was successful beyond measure, beyond our wildest hopes.

This handbook is inspired by the teachers who hear about this idea and want to try it themselves. They contact me by email, or track me down on social media. They often ask for a top-five list of ways to get started, for gear requirements, parent letters and reading lists. They wonder if this commitment to outdoor learning could possibly fly in their setting, with their students. We offer here what we've learned from our experiences. We've organized the book to address issues in the order you might approach them as you plan your own nature-based programming. Following these sections are three seasonal vignettes describing what the days in the forest looked like for my kindergarteners. Finally there is a section of encouragement followed by a series of case studies that detail the Forest Day programs of three New England kindergartens, including the perspectives of administrators and parents. First, though, let me tell you how Meg and I got started.

How It First Started

I grew up in rural New Hampshire, Meg in suburban New York. Meg's path took her to college in Vermont, mine to Chicago. We both spent time out West — Meg teaching skiing in Wyoming, while I taught preschool in Seattle and northern Alaska. Meg pursued work in politics and non-profits, and I became a kindergarten teacher. Both of us settled in Vermont and met when Meg pivoted professionally towards education and interned in my classroom in Quechee. We both had active childhoods with special wild-spaces. We didn't stop playing as adults and our mutual passion to share wonder and joy with children clarified as we spent time outdoors with our students, and later with our own growing families.

In the spring of 2013, after viewing the documentary *School's Out*, I was inspired to take my class outside. Encouraged by my principal, Amos Kornfeld, I sought Meg's help in getting this idea off the ground. Together we attended a course at Antioch University New England,

> We went to the woods to be better teachers and students, to fill our days with more enthusiasm and authenticity.

part of their Nature-based Early Childhood Education Certificate program. Our plan to give our students the gifts of nature took shape as a one-day-per-week immersion in the forest adjacent to our school.

Forest Fridays began with our Kindergartners in the fall of 2013. With initial funding support from The Wellborn Ecology Fund, Vermont Community Foundation and The Byrne Foundation, Meg joined me and my students each week for a day in the forest.

In our first year we learned a lot. We built some infrastructure: a latrine, a debris shelter and a fire circle. We navigated a balance between student-directed and teacher-directed activity. Together with our students we determined boundaries for rough and tumble play, tree-climbing, stream-wading and more. We exercised our tolerance for cold weather, our respect for the creatures of the woods and our responsibilities to each other and our space.

Our Results

People noticed. Parents, grandparents and toddling siblings joined us. The press even came (in the wrong shoes) one drippy March day. The idea resonated. Soon teachers near and far were getting in touch. As of this writing, in 2018, we count dozens of classrooms across the country that follow a similar model. Forest Day at the Ottauquechee School is now five years old, passed along to two new teachers and a new principal. Meg and I, while mothering our young children, have taken on supporting roles, assisting teachers on outdoor days, facilitating professional development in schools, leading workshops and teaching courses to help others initiate their own forest days. We've learned heaps along the way, much of it from mentors around the region who have been doing this kind of work far longer than ourselves. We hope this handbook honors what we've learned and contributes to your feeling capable of leading children in wild spaces.

Our Message to You

The first (and last!) message we wish to share is encouragement. Try it. Just try it. If you find joy in nature, if you find inspiration, wonder, calm or awe...trust that when you bring your students out, they will too.

If you find joy in nature, trust that when you bring your students out, they will find it too.

Why?

What we know by observation is supported by research: play in natural and wild spaces is good for kids. It is good for their social development, their motor development, their academic development and for the growth of elusive "soft skills:" grit, perseverance, confidence, creativity, teamwork and resilience. But why we take our students to the woods is best summarized by one word: joy. Not the flat ease of playing video-games or the brief giddiness of unwrapping candy, but the deep joyfulness of toes-in-mud, creature-in-hand, leap-over-roots and sunshine-on-cheeks. The joy of accomplishment, the joy of wonder, the joy of settling cozily in your small place within a big world. We want to give this joy to our children, and so we head to the forest. This handbook describes one way to bring a group of young students to a wild space. Each section covers an area whose importance has emerged through our years of teaching public school kindergartners in the woods beside our school. There are many ways to bring the joy of nature to children. But the first is to simply bring the children to the nature. Take those few steps out the door, and then if you'd like some ideas to take you a bit further, read on.

Why we take our students to the woods is best summarized by one word: joy. The deep joyfulness of toes-in-mud, creature-in-hand, leap-over-roots and sunshine-on-cheeks.

read

A Sense of Wonder
(Rachel Carson, 1965, 1998, HarperCollins)

Balanced and Barefoot: How Unrestricted Outdoor Play Makes for Strong, Confident and Capable Children
(Angela J Hanscom, 2016, New Harbinger)

Last Child in the Woods
(Richard Louv, 2005, Algonquin)

Childhood and Nature: Design Principles for Educators
(David Sobel, 2008, Stenhouse Publishing)

Choosing a Forest Classroom

When we commit to spending a full day outdoors each week we invite nature to be a teaching partner. Any outdoor space—field, farm or forest—offers a dynamic, rich environment that is more complex than any classroom we could design indoors. Most of what you need is already there. An outdoor classroom will be dictated by what is available. Some schools may have a forest or field that is nicely suited for a class to use, others may need to partner with a local landowner, conservation organization or park. Even if an outdoor classroom is small and simple we feel that making a commitment to the outdoors will enrich student experience. More on what we have done to enhance our forest classroom in the "infrastructure" and "gear" chapters—here we will focus on what nature has already built for us.

do:

commit – Think of this space as an extension of your indoor classroom, rather than a field trip destination. Allowing your students frequent access to the same place outdoors builds a different relationship than one-off visits. So commit to spending time in your space so often it settles in your students' psyche just as your classroom library, block area or meeting circle do.

water – If it is possible to include natural water features in your outdoor space, do. We find they are so compelling for our students. Water offers a thousand lessons over the seasons, and unfailingly draws children into experimentation, becoming your science lab with very little adult effort.

topography – We find having hills, ledges, depressions and slopes to be very useful. Look at your space with an eye towards elevation changes. For gross motor activities, science experiments or creating a natural stage, a hillside is a great feature to include in your space.

distance from school – Situating yourself away from the school building provides many advantages. One is that when the distance discourages frequent returns inside, it honors the outdoor space as complete. A distance also allows for natural transitions between inside and outside. Space for muscles to warm up on the way out, and space for minds to consolidate and organize on the way in.

ask yourself:

How frequently will you visit your outdoor site? Weekly, monthly? And for how long? A full day? A morning? An afternoon?

What will this space look like in all your seasons?

Is there shelter from the types of weather you can expect in your area, snow, rain...even sun?

How do you supervise students during water play?

What effect will your students have on the inhabitants of the pond/stream?

What will your slopes look like throughout the seasons?

What expectations do you want to have about behavior on steep sections, with an eye towards seasonal changes?

Will you travel the same path both going out and coming in?

What routines will you create based on the travel from inside to outside?

How can you capitalize on the distance, what gross motor and observational skills or chores and responsibilities will take place between inside and outside?

do:

risks – It is essential to consider the features of your space that present risks to your students. Risks in this case are dangers that are within your students' ability to understand and avoid, whether this is through rule following (we walk single file on the bridge over the stream), or by group problem solving (we noticed there was a broken branch at eye level, so we filed it down.) As the responsible adult you should have in mind the risks that present themselves in your space.

hazards – Hazards are dangers that cannot reasonably be confronted by your students. Ground-nesting bees on your trail? Poison-ivy throughout your site? Abandoned well-holes? Where the possibility for harm outweighs the opportunity for learning you must mitigate the danger.

ask yourself:

How could you develop a routine for students finding and confronting risks independently?

How do you share with all responsible adults the risks you have and how you handle teachable moments with students?

Are there a set of common risks in your area that you purposefully want to teach your students about each year?

Are there local experts who can review your space with you? Think about arborists, scout leaders, botanists, adventure guides, farmers, foresters, etcetera.

Can you involve parents in your work mitigating hazards?

read

Risk and Adventure in Early Years Outdoor Play
(Sara Knight, 2013, Sage Publications)

Establishing a Nature-Based Preschool
(Rachel A. Larimore, 2011, National Association for Interpretation)

Cultivating Outdoor Classrooms: Designing and Implementing Child-Centered Learning Environments
(Eric M. Nelson, 2012, Redleaf Press)

remember

Don't worry if you don't have acres of forest on your school property—head out into what you have available. No matter what your space looks like you will have precipitation, sunshine, plants and creatures. Part of taking your class outdoors is helping your students find a connection with the place where they live. When we embrace and value our place enough to spend this much time in it, students will learn to embrace and value their environment.

Routines

Having a structure for our day helps teachers, and students, know what to expect. We aspire to a rhythm that balances independent and group times, and teacher-led and student-directed activities. When we do this, we find we are able to take advantage of all the learning benefits the forest offers. Over our years in the woods with kindergartners we have settled into a routine that we begin teaching on our first day outside. It mirrors our inside schedule in some ways, while still allowing lots of space for free play, and quieter connecting with nature. We have indicated approximate lengths of each section of our day below, but one of the benefits of committing to a full day outdoors is that the teachers have the freedom to adjust the day. We tend to follow the same sequence week to week but the length of routines varies. The structure simplifies planning — we rely on nature and our routines to lead much of the day, while focusing our planning on weekly themes and lessons.

We rely on nature and our routines to lead much of the day.

do:

active movement – Whether it is a fifteen minute hike up a hill or a jog on a trail, allowing your students to warm up their bodies first thing helps with focus later on, and in cold weather keeps the blood flowing as they transition outside.

(15 min)

sit-spots – On our second or third visit to our space in the fall we have our students find their own "Sit-Spot." They will revisit this same spot every time we are in the forest. Anything goes as long as students are interacting with nature, not each other, so some observe, some build, some turn sticks into instruments. The Sit-Spot is a contemplative way to begin the day and gives the students a home base that is safe, secure and theirs alone.

(15 min)

morning meeting – We loosely follow a Responsive Classroom model, just as we do indoors. We start with a greeting, often inspired by nature, and then share around the circle about what has changed since our last visit to the woods. We do an activity, often movement based, and then end by checking the temperature and reflecting on any safety or schedule highlights for the day.

(20 min)

free play – While students design their own endeavors, we also typically have some offerings facilitated by teachers: cooking, gathering expeditions, site-improvement work, tracking, etc.

(60 min)

ask yourself:

Do you want to lead students in a sensory game before heading into the natural space?

Might a song make a good start to your day?

Do you want to pre-choose great spots for your students and label the choices, or let them find places on their own?

How could students mark their sit-spots?

Should you sketch a map so you can remember the spots to help forgetful students?

How can you set the tone for your day?

Do you want to make oral story-telling part of your morning meeting?

Are there short movement based activities that support your themes or lessons?

How might you carry forward threads of play and work from one forest day to the next?

How have you explicitly indicated how adults observe play?

Do adults model work (cooking, stacking wood, building, etc.) during play?

Do adults join student play? Will you add loose parts and tools to encourage play to connect with classroom learning?

do:

snack – We regroup around the fire for a hearty snack. Especially in the colder months getting enough calories at snack can really make a difference for the rest of the day.

30 min

lessons – We split into groups and lead small group lessons and activities. Inherently inspired by the seasons and the weather, these are also coordinated with our classroom curricula: math, literacy, science and social studies.

45 min

lunch – We gather around the firepit and share what we have cooked as well as eat our own lunches. We often read-aloud or tell a story during lunch.

30 min

free play – Before heading back inside we send the kids for a bit more play. Sometimes we lead group games or expeditions for those interested.

30 min

closing circle – We meet for one last time around the fire and have some ritual of thanks and bidding goodbye to the forest as we douse the flames with water.

10 min

ask yourself:

Can your class bake a snack the day before your forest day to bring outside?

How can movement be part of academic practice and exploration?

What natural materials can you use for math or literacy?

How will you manage participation? Will students rotate to every group, or will students make choices?

Will your class eat all together or spread out in smaller groups?

Are there any recurring jobs (cleaning up space, washing dishes, etc.) that could be assigned to a rotating crew?

Are students revisiting ideas from the "lessons" section in the second round of free play?

Do you want to revisit any Morning Meeting activities?

read

Sharing Nature with Children
(Joseph Cornell, 1979, Dawn Publications)

The Morning Meeting Book
(Carol Davis and Roxann Kriete, 2014,
Center for Responsive Schools)

Coyote's Guide to Connecting With Nature
(Jon Young, Ellen Haas, Evan McGown,
2010, OWLink Media)
(see chapter three: Core Routines of
Nature Connection)

Nature Kindergartens and Forest Schools,
2nd Edition
(Clare Warden, 2012, Mindstretchers)

remember

We have been best served when we set out with an intentional sequence of routines in our minds right at the beginning of the year and spend the first few forest days building up these routines. Your rhythms may be different. Our planning is guided by the belief that play and exploration are the context for learning for young children. We want to structure their time outdoors to allow our students to get deeply engaged with inventions and investigations of their own design. We want routines to hold space for us to demonstrate skills, model habits and share facts that promote our students' development and understanding of the world around them.

> "It's like Forest Friday is a treasure."
> – Kindergartner
> Marion Cross School,
> Vermont

Role of the Adult

The responsibility to keep students safe when we lead them to wild spaces is always on our minds. Always. Beyond that is where we find ourselves working hard to be purposeful about our facilitation of outdoor play and learning. We gain a lot by watching and listening to our students, rather than doing and telling. When we understand what our students are thinking, attempting or wondering our responses are targeted, efficient, and effective.

The outdoors invites us to use nature as a teaching partner, and to step back from the scripted style popular in classroom teaching today. Trust your students!

We gain a lot by watching and listening to our students.

do:

protect – To keep your students safe in a wild space there are a few common sense steps to take. First is to survey the space for hazards. Standing or leaning dead trees, barbed wire, old wells, sharp and rusted debris, poisonous plants(poison ivy!), aggressive wildlife(bees!), and rivers are all among site hazards that should be mitigated or removed before bringing children to the space. There are likely more that are specific to your space. Next you need plans to supervise students, as well as how you approach known risks (the fire-pit for example.) We count our students every ten minutes and at every transition, which means we know where each student is and what activity they are engaged in. Counting in alphabetical order prevents miscounting, and immediately alerts you as to who is out of sight.

model – Rather than teaching every routine and skill, the adults can simply do the desired behavior. When we want our students to begin journaling, we bring out our own journals and share our entries each week. When we want students to rake leaves away from the fire-pit, we start doing it ourselves, with a few extra rakes nearby. We expect our students to do as we do.

provision – Provisioning is the idea that we provide some props to encourage the develop-ment of concepts and skills. Sometimes we have certain curriculum goals in mind, sometimes we follow cues from student interest when we pick loose parts to add to our space. We keep it simple and open-ended. A few old dishes can encourage a world of pretend play. Access to a variety of thermometers for a few weeks promotes engagement with numbers, temperatures, and weather.

ask yourself:

Who can you ask to review your site with you?

How do you communicate your supervision plans with your staff and volunteers?

Do you want to have risk assessments on hand for your space?

How will you communicate to all adults involved what the expectations are during quiet times and play times? Are you playing during play times? Are you quiet during quiet times?

How will you monitor that you yourself are demonstrating the habits you hope to see in your children?

How will students want to play with what you have brought to the space?

Can you allow open-ended play with these items?

Should you teach the tool first, or let students explore the tool first?

Does this prop have a fixed or obvious use, or can it be used in a variety of play scenarios?

do:

plan – We use our forest day routines to our advantage in that learning goals are embedded in everyday work that we teach once, and benefit from all year long. Routines like sharing observations, reporting on the temperature, and rotating jobs, once taught, do not require weekly planning, but do provide weekly opportunities for language, math, and science work. Then we have a few specific chunks of the day to which we can dedicate our planning efforts. We balance seasonal inspiration from our forest, with proscribed grade level curricular goals. We use natural materials and lesson design to support the ongoing work in the classroom.

extend – When we are doing the best by young children we are providing lots of time for free play, and we are learning from their play. We pick up on current interests and activities and use those themes as foundations for learning throughout all domains. We ask open-ended questions, provide open-ended materials, and furnish tools, media and experts that expand and deepen their experiences.

ask yourself:

What outdoor seasons best fit your grade level science units?

What non-fiction books can you gather which are connected with your outdoor resources?

What work can you get your routines to do for you?

How can you echo indoor lessons with louder, more active lessons outdoors?

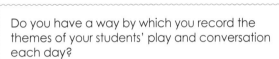

Do you have a way by which you record the themes of your students' play and conversation each day?

How do you communicate to all the adults the differences between supervising, directing and extending play?

How can themes that develop outdoors stretch indoors and vice versa?

read

Lens on Outdoor Learning
(Wendy Banning and Ginny Sullivan, 2011, Redleaf)

The Outdoor Classroom in Practice, Ages 3-7
(Karen Constable, 2014, Routledge)

Nature Preschools and Forest Kindergartens: The Handbook for Outdoor Learning
(David Sobel, 2015, Redleaf)

Fascination of Fire: Charcoal, Fascination of Earth: Wood, Fascination of Water: Puddles, Fascination of Air: Wind
(Claire Warden, 2012, 2013, Mindstretchers)

Talking and Thinking Floorbooks: An Approach to Consultation, Observation, Planning and Assessment in Children's Learning (Claire Warden, 1995, Mindstretchers)

remember

The fear of hazards is cited frequently as a challenge to taking students into wild spaces. **Our best advice is just to try taking your students out.** Just try. Trust your gut; if something makes you nervous, express that to your students and work through it together. It is very likely that together you will build a confidence in their ability to keep themselves safe.

Invite parents, local experts and administrators to do risk evaluations with you. Consider what students gain by confronting risk, whether these risks are connected with an opportunity worth providing. We think yes! Be intentional about how you involve yourself (or do not involve yourself) in the play and work of your students outdoors. How can you allow them to pull you into their learning, rather than you pushing them into yours?

Infrastructure

When we plan to spend a full day (or more) outdoors each week throughout the seasons there are a series of logistical challenges we must confront. As much as we can, we create infrastructure to meet these challenges together as a class. Each fall we extend our time outdoors as we build the infrastructure we require. Each spring we dismantle structures, leaving the woods as we found it (mostly), and allowing next year's class to create their own space. We keep it simple, but there are a handful of projects that we've found essential for our time outdoors with young children. The items below are listed in the order in which we develop them in the fall with a new class.

We keep it simple.

do:

benches – We don't always sit on benches, but having a place to sit is welcoming to students not yet accustomed to the forest, helps students focus during discussions and meals, and keeps our rears off the snow during the winter months. Our first class built benches with a volunteer using logs cut lengthwise with a chainsaw. Other classes use stumps (that can be mobile, or can be sunk in the ground), or bring in some lumber.

fire pit – Having a central spot around which to gather, talk, eat and cook is a natural start for an outdoor space. We conferred with our local fire department, and keep a standing permit on file, as well as calling each morning to register our campfire. We dug a very deep hole, down to mineral-earth (non-combustible - think gravel, not soil or leaf debris). We lined with rock, back-filled with sand, and then made a boundary ring with logs. We added a tripod, from which to hang a dutch oven. Each year students dig out the pit, clear away plant material, and learn the rules and responsibilities of having a fire.

shelter – We haven't ended up using a shelter too much for ourselves, but for our firewood and gear we've found it important to have protection from the rain. We lash logs (not rotten!) to trees and stretch tarps to provide a place for backpacks and firewood to stay dry. A shelter like this can also make for a nice play or reading spot, so we make it big enough for people and keep it fairly clear.

ask yourself:

Who can you enlist to help with building projects? Parent volunteers? Local businesses?

How likely are you to have visitors to your outdoor space, and will other groups want to use the space? Does this change how many seats you will want to build?

Can students design their own seating?

If a fire pit is out of the question, could a portable self-contained metal pit work? Would a self-contained Kelly Kettle work?

How will you solicit donations of firewood each year?

What are your explicit rules for having a fire and how do you communicate these to both children and adults?

Can you involve your fire department in teaching fire safety at your outdoor setting?

If you are a tentative builder, who can you enlist to help?

How do you test your structures to ensure safety?

Will you use a manmade impervious roofing material, or will you research a natural cover technique?

do:

latrine – We can't stay out in the woods very long until we've developed a way to toilet in the forest. The latrine is a structure we create anew each year. Children identify the problem, and help to build latrine walls by lashing fresh limbs as cross-beams around a tight stand of trees and then leaning more limbs upright to make walls. Students also haul a five-gallon bucket with toilet seat up to the latrine each morning (an adult hauls it back inside each afternoon). Others have hung tarps to create a private space, or purchased a pop-up latrine tent.

loose parts – Nature provides a variety of props, but sometimes, especially if you've used the same site for years, it can seem that all the acorns have been stored away, and all the sticks have been used at the fire pit. We do occasionally furnish items to the space. Tree slices (or "cookies"), limbs cut to manageable sizes (1'-3'), local leaves and seeds are among collections we've brought to our space. You may also use non-natural items, such as discarded baking tins and utensils for a mud-kitchen or music-tree. Lengths of twine, paint mixing sticks and durable child-sized tools are among items we've also seen teachers add to their outdoor space.

ask yourself:

Can you dig a pit toilet in your space?

How can you store toilet paper so that you always have it with you outside?

Is there a way students know that the latrine is occupied?

Is there a designated waiting-for-the-bathroom spot?

Are your students able to manuever snowpants or rain-gear on and off themselves, or will they need help?

Is there a local hardware or agricultural supply store that might donate items?

read

Forest and Nature Schools in Canada: A Head Heart, Hands Approach to Outdoor Learning
(Rebecca Carruthers and Den Hoed, 2014, Forest Schools Canada)

Loose Parts: Inspiring Play in Young Children
(Lisa Daly, 2014, Redleaf)

Nature Play & Learning Places. Creating and Managing Places Where Children Engage with Nature
(Robin Moore, 2014 Natural Learning Initiative and National Wildlife Federation)

remember

Some of the items in this section are daunting challenges for teachers, and yet all those we've helped have been surprised at how smoothly the solutions proceed once they are underway. For example, toileting in the woods has, in our experience, resulted in fewer issues than in the stall bathrooms inside. We've found our local firefighters to be willing partners in supporting our weekly pit fires. Easing into extended outdoor time took us years; pick one structural challenge at a time and solve it before moving on to the next. One day you'll find you have no reason at all to go back inside!

Gear

We want outdoor time to be as easy as possible, and never a burden on families. We want our students to be comfortable so that they can work and play hard in nature. To that end we've acquired some gear through donation, thrift store purchases and using grant funding. Local businesses have been eager to partner up to provide items for children, you may find the same if you reach out. While we ask students to dress in extra layers through the colder weather, we don't ask that they have anything more than what a student would bring for a regular recess. In our list below are the items we've found prudent to invest in for the class. The last set of gear pertains to cooking outdoors, and suggests a few items that might simplify the process.

We want our students to be comfortable so that they can work and play hard in nature.

do:

rainpants – Waterproof overalls keep students clean, dry and warm throughout the school year. Children and adults wear them to feel confident kneeling and sitting on the ground, as well as to stay dry when it is raining, or when the snow is melting. While snow-pants are best on a cold winter's day, rain-pants are great on any other day except for the warmest days in fall and spring.

rubber boots – Like overalls, rubber boots serve us well except in the coldest weather. With rubber boots children can most easily explore all the muddy, wet and slushy places that are often the most compelling.

wool lined boots – Not all winter boots are created equal, and we've found that having a collection of great boots helps fill in the gaps. Keeping feet dry and warm goes a long way in keeping a kid warm, so we are on the look-out to upgrade boots when we can. Some classrooms have purchased an entire class set, others just keep a number of selected used pairs on hand.

ask yourself:

How many different sizes will you need to outfit your group? Can you color code by size? Can classes share if they go out on different days?

How will you store the pants so that they can dry between uses?

Is there a place outside your classroom to leave rubber boots, minimizing the muddy footprints?

Can you collect donations of rubber boots as students grow out of them?

Can you request donations of quality used boots?

Is there a parent who can keep an eye out at local thrift stores for gear for your class?

Can you start a collection of wool socks to lend on forest days?

do:

mittens – Like winter boots, there is a variety of mittens and gloves, from fairly useless to phenomenal. In our cold setting we prefer lined, waterproof mittens, and nothing less. (Polyester gloves are the stuff of nightmares!) Quality mittens are another item we keep on hand to fill in gaps. There are companies who make long, waterproof varieties, but we've also done all right just inheriting pairs and keeping an eye out at thrift stores.

neck-warmers – For the coldest days we've found neckwarmers to be pretty helpful in keeping the warmth from escaping our coats, and for keeping cheeks and noses warm. We've taken to sewing our own fleece neck-warmers as an indoor project when we are kept inside by temperatures below the school cut-off.

cookware – We have found that having a cooking grate, a cast-iron grill/griddle and dutch oven have served us well for a pretty complete variety of cooking needs. From boiling sap to baking cakes, from sauteing vegetables to flipping pancakes, these three cooking tools have worked great. We have a metal camp-mug for each student. These are used for water, as well as for any item we prepare in the woods, from hot-drinks to apple-crisp to stone-soup.

ask yourself:

How do you check the quality of your students' preparedness before you head outside?

Is there a volunteer who might share sewing expertise for a few afternoons to help children make their own neck-warmers?

Are there other weather related projects you can prepare for days when extreme weather forces you inside?

Can you leave any of your cookware at your outdoor space to minimize carrying heavy or dirty items frequently?

How can cookware be cleaned outdoors? Are there frequently used utensils of dishes that can be reusable to cut down on waste?

read

Forest Kindergartens:
The Cedarsong Way
(Erin Kenny, 2013, Cedarsong Nature School)

There's No Such Thing as Bad Weather
(Linda Akeson McGurk, 2017, Simon and Schuster)

Wild Play: Parenting Adventures
in the Great Outdoors
(David Sobel, 2018, Green Writer's Press)

remember

There are many ways to fill out your gear supply. Often teachers can solicit grant funding or direct donations of gear. Local outfitters may be willing to give you a discount, especially if you are making a large order. Of course young children grow out of much of these things before they wear out, so the hand-me-down path is usually quite fruitful. Be on the look-out to take advantage of volunteer skills as well.

A Fall Day...

active movement to our space – Early on in the year, students follow us up the trail, we pause to point out things we notice on the trail, or to stop to focus on on sense… "Can you smell the stream?" "I wonder what I am hearing."

sit-spots – At this point students are likely spending ten minutes at their sit-spots.

morning meeting – Students share what they've noticed is different in our woods space - the air is drier, there are more leaves on the ground, walking in the leaf litter was louder. Now, before the snow flies, is the time to gather kindling for our winter fires. For our morning meeting activity students are sent to gather ten "chickadee sticks," sticks the size a chickadee might wrap its toes around. When they gather back around the fire-pit we spend some time having the students show how they know they have ten. Have they counted by twos? or made two groups of five? are there other groupings to ten? Then we all count the handfuls up by tens, as we add them to our firewood pile nearby. We check the temperature and find that it is a few degrees cooler than last week, but it isn't below freezing yet.

free play – In the fall we find our students spend time climbing the ropes secured over rock faces behind our fire pit, or collecting fallen limbs for shelter building. Lean-tos pop up all around and many children engage in pretend play, often focused on animal activity and stories. At the fire-pit a teacher works with a few kids to prepare and bake apple crisp. Students cut apples with butter knives and sprinkle oats, sugar and cinnamon into the dutch oven.

snack – The apple crisp isn't quite ready, so we snack on the muffins students made in class the afternoon before. We chat about what we were working on during free-play and point out some of the interesting things we observed about our space and each other.

lessons – In the fall we are often able to run three or more teacher-directed stations in a morning. In a group of six or seven, students collect natural manipulatives to create math challenge problems for their friends. For example Bobby gains the attention of his peers around the circle and spreads out three acorns, two beech leaves and a rock. he describes his collection and asks, "How many altogether?" He calls on his classmates and we work together to prove our answers. Sally has a different idea, she shows her collection of ten things, oak leaves and pine cones, and then tells a story of a red squirrel wandering by and taking the pine cones for his dinner and asks "How many things are left?" In another station students settle onto a fallen tree, and take turns acting out the Three Billy Goats Gruff, a story they are studying in the classroom. They retell and sequence, taking charge of being storytellers and performers.

"The forest classroom offers so many incredible opportunities for practicing persistence, creative problem solving, and building self confidence."
– MaryKay Cronin
Kindergarten teacher
Albert Bridge School, Vermont

At yet another station students play a predator prey chase game that requires syllable counting. The coyote (teacher) is only steps behind the rabbits (students) who can only take as many steps toward their warren as there are syllables in the words they take turns saying. "Evergreen!" shouts Joe, "Ev-er-green! That's three!" his classmates squeal as they turn and take three steps away from the coyote, hot on their tracks with "de-cid-u-ous!"

lunch – We gather back at the fire-pit and students pick through their lunch-bags. The chefs from earlier in the day help serve the apple-crisp. When everyone has settled into munching a teacher tells an adapted Three Billy Goats Gruff about The Three Salamanders Tough who are waylaid by a greedy raccoon as they try to cross the stream in our woods, taking suggestions from the kids around the campfire as to what the characters might say.

play – Students pack up their lunches and scoot off into the woods for more play before we must return to the school. A group, who usually doesn't play together inside, is noticed acting out the Three Billy Goats Gruff near a debris shelter. Some return to building, others to running between trees and calling for help to move a large fallen limb near a path.

closing – A few students are disappointed to be called back to the fire-pit. "Can't we stay out longer?" We collect all our bits and pieces and, after singing a thank you and good-bye to the forest, a teacher generously douses the fire. We hike back to school, stomp dirt from our treads, and then flop on the classroom floor to record the story of our day on our Forest Day blog.

"Children with special needs drew much from the peace, beauty, and adventure of the forest. Without the confinement of walls and desks, their minds were freed to hear the comforting sounds of nature that called them to learn of life through experience and observation. They blossomed and matured in the forest."

– Nancy Cardenuto
Special Educator
Ottauquechee School, Vermont

Selected Academic Learning Standards

CCSS.ELA-LITERACY.RL.K.9	With prompting and support, compare and contrast the adventures and experiences of characters in familiar stories.
CCSS.MATH.CONTENT.K.CC.A.1	Count to 100 by ones and by tens.
CCSS.MATH.CONTENT.K.CC.B.4.B	Understand that the last number name said tells the number of objects counted. The number of objects is the same regardless of their arrangement or the order in which they were counted.
NGSS.K-ESS2-1	Use and share observations of local weather conditions to describe patterns over time.
CCSS.MATH.CONTENT.K.OA.A.1	Represent addition and subtraction with objects, fingers, mental images, drawings, sounds (e.g., claps), acting out situations, verbal explanations, expressions, or equations.
CCSS.ELA-LITERACY.RF.K.2.B	Count, pronounce, blend, and segment syllables in spoken words.
CCSS.ELA-LITERACY.RL.K.2	With prompting and support, retell familiar stories, including key details.

A Winter Day...

active movement to our space – Winter temperature fluctuations and our trampling of the snowy path have presented us with a formidable challenge - the trail is sheer ice when we return from mid-winter break. We have a brief pause and plan while we look up the hill. Some students grab sticks to use as ice-picks, others preemptively drop to all fours, while others jump off the trail and stamp in crusty, undisturbed snow. Soon most have realized that off-trail walking proves the best method.

sit-spots – It may take as much as twice as long as usual for some to reach the firepit, but we all arrive eventually and after dropping off supplies, everyone heads to their sit-spots. Hot and winded from the hike we settle in for fifteen or so minutes of quiet observation. The snow makes comfortable recliners for some, or the chance to dig and build for others.

morning meeting – When we start with a greeting we begin standing and exchange goofy jumps as we say good morning around the circle, to get the blood flowing. Today when we share our observations we hear about the sound of the ice, the brittleness of sticks, and the mystery of our breaths in the cold. Lest our bodies begin to cool down we do an active counting activity, during which we have assigned big movements to the evens, fives and tens. By the time we've counted to fifty we've squatted, jumped and raised-the-roof. Our morning message question asked students to think about how they adapt to winter. We note their answers, on display in the way they are dressed and the ways we change our routines in the cold. When we check the temperature we find it is 22°F.

"In the forest I pretend to be a red fox named Melody."
– Second Grader
Sharon Elementary School, Vermont

free play – We find the children stay closer and in larger groups in the cold weather. More than half carve an icy slide down the nearby slope, and we spot up to ten going down together. They laugh and slip on the way down as a train of otters, and then shout and wait for each other to get organized at the top once again. Another group finds they can cut crust chunks from the top of snow in a small clearing and they begin to stack them into an igloo. An adult joins their work, following directions from a budding foreman. At the fire a few students help mix ingredients in the dutch oven for a simple macaroni and cheese. One of these children begins to complain her hands are cold. We bundle her up a bit tighter and after some jumping jacks we send her off with a "Best Buddy" to play follow-the-leader.

snack – We call everyone in once the cheese has melted, and in addition to hearty muffins, we decide to serve up the warm mac-and-cheese. It might be too cold to take our mittens off for lunch in the woods today, so we'll have a big warm snack and stay out as long as we can.

lessons – Half the class heads off into the woods on a tracking expedition. We can often find deer beds if we follow the tracks long enough. We can play games as we walk and point out interesting phenomena...how did all these little hemlock twigs end up on top of the snow? The others stay back near the fire and after listening to a picture-book about what we can find under and over the snow, we play an "Under the Snow" game. While students close their eyes the teacher selects a few to hide under a white sheet. Those remaining guess at who and how many are "under the snow." Some students rely on their social bearings to figure out who is missing, others start to do subtraction to determine the number of hidden friends. Those hiding try to mask their shape in acrobatic ways, and certainly don't make a peep, lest any over-the-snow predators suss them out!

lunch – 22°F has proven too cold to take off our mittens to eat outside, so we'll push lunch off until we return to the classroom. Instead we gather for more play and the offering of some teacher led games.

play – One teacher hides a raccoon stuffed animal in the crook of a tree and children race into the woods to find him in his winter den. Some use her footprints to track the hiding place, others ask for direction clues. Can they remember which way is North in our woods a few weeks after we learned, or can they read the moss on the trees for clues? Other students head back to the otter slide.

closing – Soon we pack up, sing our song of thanks to the forest and douse the fire. Our students cannot contain their eagerness to be the lucky ones kissed by the hissing steam as it rises in the breeze. Our "fire chief" (we now have a variety of student jobs built into our outdoor day) calls the fire department to let them know our fire is out. Once back in the school building we hang up our clothes, warm our toes by rubbing them on the rug, and settle in with our lunches. While eating, we develop a chart comparing our adaptations for winter with the deer, squirrel and raccoons we know are in our woods. We also create a blog post about the day, noting that some classes didn't even get recess because of the cold weather and windchill...and we spent two and a half hours outside!

"Bumps were invented for boys to slide on."
– Fifth Grader
Sharon Elementary
School, Vermont

Selected Academic Learning Standards

NGSS.K-ESS3-2	Ask questions to obtain information about the purpose of weather forecasting to prepare for, and respond to, severe weather.
NGSS.K-LS1-1	Use observations to describe patterns of what plants and animals (including humans) need to survive.
CCSS.MATH.CONTENT.K.OA.A.2	Solve addition and subtraction word problems, and add and subtract within 10, e.g., by using objects or drawings to represent the problem.
CCSS.ELA-LITERACY.RL.K.10	Actively engage in group reading activities with purpose and understanding.
CCSS.ELA-LITERACY.SL.K.4	Describe familiar people, places, things, and events and, with prompting and support, provide additional detail.
CCSS.ELA-LITERACY.RI.K.2	With prompting and support, identify the main topic and retell key details of a text.
CCSS.ELA-LITERACY.W.K.6	With guidance and support from adults, explore a variety of digital tools to produce and publish writing, including in collaboration with peers.

A Spring Day...

active movement to our space – As the weather warms we are rewarded for all the effort in the fall and winter, first building our outdoor infrastructure and then trekking there through challenging weather. In the spring we are strong, the hike is easy, and the forest classroom and routines are comfortable. We can send the students to follow their own path to their sit-spots and enjoy their independence.

sit-spots – Sit-Spots may last twenty minutes. Now students opt-in to bringing journals with them, and have their own set of colored pencils with which to illustrate while settling into the woods each week.

morning meeting – When we call in the students those first to arrive begin sharing their journals if they want to. Once we are all gathered we greet each other and note the changes since our last visit. Change is fast and furious in the spring. Week to week buds turn to leaves, the stream from a rush to intermittent puddles. We note the sounds, smells and textures. We revisit a favorite activity: "Disappear." While the teacher closes her eyes and counts to four, everyone else hides. She opens her eyes and calls out who can be seen from her stationary vantage point. Then, when she calls "Pop!" those still hidden jump out from behind trees and stumps, shocking us with how well hidden they were, while being still so close. Our students have learned to be woodland animals capable of scampering out of sight at a moment's notice, aware of the teacher's perspective, as well as the space taken up by their own bodies. We predict the temperature before checking the thermometer and find that the students are often within five degrees after a school year's worth of experience.

> "Teacher, can I sing? This is the best day ever."
> – Kindergartner Ottauquechee School, Vermont

free play – Play in the spring often involves the stream. Kindergartners mostly want to clear the water's path, though some become interested in damming the flow. Students group together for building projects and pretend play scenarios. There are also creatures to be found and there is a lot of discussion and work around enjoying, and protecting, the salamanders and snails that share our forest. With the warm weather it becomes easier to cook more elaborate recipes, so a few students mix up dough, and throughout the playtime, all students visit the fire to roast their own bread on a stick. Students also cut fruit for a salad.

snack – We eat our stick-bread and fruit salad with brook-rinsed but still muddy fingers and are quickly ready to split into teacher directed groups.

lessons – The kindergarteners are working on a unit about identifying and using tools of measurement. In one station today we make our own balance scales with short boards and logs. Pairs of students work together first to collect items to be weighed, then to make a balanced scale, and lastly to experiment with different found items. Weight, they discover, is not always in a direct relationship with size, and they work to balance a rock on one side, with sticks on the other. Soon they eagerly try to find things equal to their own weight. In their next station, partnered up again and armed with stopwatches, they experiment with how far they can move in ten seconds. The timer calls out a type of movement: Crawling! Skipping! Running! Slithering! and then gives a countdown before starting the ten second stopwatch. "Stop!!!" The mover turns to see how far he's gotten from his partner. They switch back and forth, experimenting with both the tool, and the relationship of time with their bodies and space.

lunch – We have a relaxing lunch in the warm woods. As the sun rises overhead, we're thankful the leaves provide some shade. A teacher reads aloud another Old Mother West Wind story, and then has the class tell it back. We recall together all the tales and characters we now know. We can discuss who might be able to get the furthest in ten seconds, and who might be the heaviest. The Merry Little Breezes are surely the lightest.

play – A few students congregate around the stump and board balances, another few ask to borrow stop watches and run to a clearing. Others return to pretend play scenarios. We stretch play for as long as possible before singing to the forest, dousing the fire, and returning to the classroom, where, monkey-like, the children partner up to check each other for ticks. They part each other's hair in a giggling ritual, body-tired and heart-full from a warm day in the woods.

"The children have been so eager, engaged, and really take responsibility out in the woods. This has built a team approach and strengthened relationships that have transferred to our class time, as well."

- Ingrid Johnson
Kindergarten teacher
Barnard Academy,
Vermont

Selected Academic Learning Standards

CCSS.ELA-LITERACY.W.K.2	Use a combination of drawing, dictating, and writing to compose informative/explanatory texts in which they name what they are writing about and supply some information about the topic.
CCSS.ELA-LITERACY.SL.K.5	Add drawings or other visual displays to descriptions as desired to provide additional detail.
CCSS.ELA-LITERACY.L.K.5.C	Identify real-life connections between words and their use (e.g., note places at school that are colorful).
CCSS.MATH.CONTENT.K.MD.A.1	Describe measurable attributes of objects, such as length or weight. Describe several measurable attributes of a single object.
CCSS.MATH.CONTENT.K.CC.A.2	Count forward beginning from a given number within the known sequence (instead of having to begin at 1).
NGSS.K-ESS2-2	Construct an argument supported by evidence for how plants and animals (including humans) can change the environment to meet their needs.
CCSS.MATH.CONTENT.K.MD.A.2	Directly compare two objects with a measurable attribute in common, to see which object has "more of"/"less of" the attribute, and describe the difference.

Try It!

An essential chapter in Jon Young's Coyote's *Guide to Connecting With Nature* yet unmentioned is "Indicators of Awareness." This chapter provides an inspiring lens for assessment of the skills and habits you will cultivate when you take your students to a wild-space with frequency and intention. Really, it's beyond skills and habits; it's character and disposition and it will send you to the woods with more resolve than anything I can write. Read the chapter. Read it and then head to the forest for a few minutes. Let those minutes stretch to hours. Watch your students; follow their passions. Stretch their muscles. All their muscles. The physical muscles, the academic muscles, the engineering muscles, the craftsy muscles, the empathy muscles. See how strong you all become. Try it.

Shush the voice in your ear that whispers "my students are older, sure this is cute for kindergartners, but sixth graders?" Yes. Sixth graders. Wrestle down the anxiety that claims you have no time to spare for such a folly as outdoor play and adventure, for learning grounded in the nature beyond our school walls. Do you know the best way to convince yourself this is important, essential and so worth it? Take your students outside. Try it.

Take recess to the woods, or even to the drainage ditch. Take the read aloud to the lawn, take your snack to the trees. Then ask your students to tell you what they see, and hear, and smell; ask them to draw it. Ask them to build something - for a fairy, for a worm, for themselves, for a classmate, for the school. Ask them to count the number of creatures in a circle a foot in diameter, count the sounds in ten minutes, count the branch whorls on a pine tree. Ask them what they would like to do with a free afternoon in this wildspace, then say: Try it.

Take your
students
outside.
Try it.

Appendix

Forest Days Case Studies

Hartland Elementary, Vermont;
Ludlow Elementary, Vermont;
Mount Lebanon Elementary,
New Hampshire

Prepared for
Antioch University New England
and the Wellborn Ecology Fund

Prepared by
PEER Associates
Primary author: Amy Powers
August 2017

ANTIOCH UNIVERSITY
NEW ENGLAND

NEW HAMPSHIRE
CHARITABLE FOUNDATION
Upper Connecticut River Mitigation and Enhancement Fund

Forest Days Case Studies
Hartland Elementary, Vermont; Ludlow Elementary, Vermont; Mount Lebanon Elementary, New Hampshire

Project Background

The goal of this evaluation project was to better understand the implementation of and potential for Forest Days programs in the early primary grades in Vermont and New Hampshire public schools. This report will serve as a companion document to the *Forest Days Handbook* currently in creation by Eliza Minucci and David Sobel.

The intended audience for this report includes:
- Teachers wishing to implement similar programs with their classes;
- Principals, school board members, and communities seeking a rationale for implementing these programs in their schools; and
- Parents who wish to understand the benefits of this type of programming for their children.

The guiding questions for this project were:
- What do Forest Days programs look like in the three communities profiled?
- In what ways do educators, parents, and administrators value Forest Days for students?
- Do educators, parents, and administrators notice benefits to Forest Days students in the areas of motivation and enthusiasm, language development, STEM learning, physical development, and executive function? (Secondary exploration: To what extent do educators, parents, and administrators notice a difference in behavior problems in students on Forest Days vs. classroom days?)
- From the perspective of educators, parents, and administrators, are Forest Days students meeting learning standards? Are they confident that Forest Days students are adequately equipped to enter the next grade level?
- What challenges and obstacles have educators, parents, and administrators observed in implementing Forest Days programming in their schools?

Case Study Teachers and Sites:
- Lauren Skilling and Amanda Soule, Hartland Elementary, Hartland, VT
- Barb Koski and Emma Eckert, Ludlow Elementary, Ludlow, VT
- Christina Wild, Mount Lebanon School, Lebanon, NH

Methods

The project began with with a brief planning phase to ensure mutual understanding of the overarching goals and to determine the timeline and personnel roles. This phase included the creation of a <u>spreadsheet that inventories and catalogues the schools/communities where Forest Days are happening in New Hampshire and Vermont</u>[2].

PEER Associates developed interview guides to use with educators, parents, and administrators in the three communities, and during a meeting of the <u>Professional Learning Community (PLC) focused on Outdoor Play and Learning</u>, PEER also conducted an on site focus group with participating educators. Evaluators also reviewed existing data sources and artifacts of the programs such as photos, weekly blog entries, and newsletters.

Interviews were recorded, and detailed field notes were taken. Interview data was analyzed qualitatively, coding interview notes for prevalent themes. A portrait of each of the three schools is presented below, followed by a cross site view of dominant themes.

---

[2] http://forestkinder.org/forest-day-classrooms (Additions to this list are welcome. Please contact Eliza Minnucci at eliza@forestkinder.org.)

Forest Days Case Studies: Hartland, Ludlow, Mount Lebanon, & Cross Cutting Findings

Case Study: Hartland Elementary School, Vermont

It's barely 9am on a January morning in Vermont, and Hartland Elementary School kindergarteners are on a mission. Crunching lunches into backpacks, stomping into giant boots, the bustling is surprisingly methodical, self-directed, and at a noticeably low volume. It's Wednesday in the Woods, and when the 30 or so children and their six accompanying adults cross the fence at the edge of the neatly mowed playing fields into the 17 acres of forested hills behind the school, their classroom is transformed.

Their usual route to this outdoor classroom is down a steep hill, using a rope strung from tree to tree as a handrail. Today, however, the class is faced with a problem. Vermont's often erratic winter weather has replaced their trail down with a sheet of ice. Before even arriving to their learning space, the class is faced with a problem-solving, team building activity whose authenticity one couldn't begin to invent in the classroom: how will we get down this hill safely together?

For the next twenty minutes the students are testing their courage, their bodies, their knowledge of the area and of winter conditions, and their understanding of who they can help and rely on. Some (including one paraprofessional!) are inching down on their bottoms; others, otter-like in their confidence, sail down on their bellies; a few rugged yet cautious ones have discovered that stomping hard will break footholds in the icy crust; and of course, a few have lost their footing altogether and are being caught by a friend or teacher. This wasn't in today's lesson plan, but as experienced place-based educators, the teachers have learned to adapt to what nature provides them and even the trip to and from the outdoor classroom can offer valuable learning opportunities.

Case Study Data Sources: Hartland Elementary School
- 4 parents, formal interviews
- 2 classroom teachers, formal interviews
- 1 Administrator, formal interview
- 1 Reading specialist, 2 classroom aids, informal conversations
- Students, informal conversations
- Full day observation of Wednesday in the Woods
- Classroom Blog

Planting the sapling

Hartland Elementary is one of about 20 schools in Vermont and New Hampshire where learning outdoors is truly integrated into the school week. A town of 3,400, Hartland lies in the Upper Valley of the Connecticut River and its elementary school serves the town's 311 preK-8th grade students, 40% of whom are free lunch eligible.

Beginning in the 2015-2016 school year, two innovative kindergarten teachers and a supportive administrator launched Wednesdays in the Woods. At the time, the teachers were part of a

Professional Learning Community (PLC) focused on Outdoor Play and Learning, and they visited other sites to glean ideas for their space and routines. They decided to organize their program as a combination of structured and unstructured time, balancing the needs of children to have boundaries with the benefits of freedom and choice that derive from self-guided learning and play. About a dozen families participated in an initial work day to build the site, which includes a large, rock-lined fire pit and a rustic lean-to. The program started small--bringing students to the outdoor site first for a half hour, then 45 minutes, and eventually building up to the full day immersion.

Spreading Branches

"Overall we've done a disservice to kids at all grade levels because there isn't that time for play. People who don't understand just think play is wasting time, but that is the way they learn--through their play. When we just have them sit at desks...we're missing out on opportunities to engage kids." With this recognition, the administrator at Hartland Elementary underscored the foundation of the many benefits afforded by outdoor, play-based learning.

And with a seemingly instinctive grasp of the research on self-directed learning, the kids, one after the next, highlight the benefit of these Wednesdays as, "I get to choose."

In a series of interviews, classroom teachers, parents, and the administrator shared their experiences with Wednesday in the Woods; its origins, workings, and most importantly, what it was doing for the kindergarteners.

Academic benefits

The mix of creative, self-directed play with the structure of "bringing the curriculum outside" is yielding results. As one teacher described, "We might not sit down at our tables and do our worksheets but we have discussions that are priceless. We bring out the curriculum in fun ways that stick with the kids and then we can make links back in the classroom. We're always saying, 'Remember that experience we had?'"

As the learning found its way home, parents took notice. "Being outside has helped her creativity when she's writing," reported one parent. "She's more able to imagine scenarios--it seems like she's more excited about imaginary play and likes to write stories about it. They keep a journal for Wednesday in the Woods, and she has carried that on at home."

Science, too, is a natural fit for the outdoor classroom. Different parents reported that "My daughter goes outside now with a much more critical eye. She really has gotten an eye for how to compare and contrast things and how to notice changes," and "I don't remember the names of all the different things in nature, so when we go play outside behind our house it's an opportunity for [my daughter] to teach me about all different flowers, leaves, trees. She so enjoys teaching me about what she learned."

Beyond the academic disciplines, interviewees recalled many stories in which students developed 21st Century Skills such as teamwork and problem solving in the authentic setting of the outdoors. The students worked together to move an enormous log, to build a shelter that kept collapsing, and create a primitive teeter-totter on which to play. And teamwork, of course, requires the development of communication skills--using words clearly, making one's voice heard, listening respectfully to others' ideas. As a parent noted, "So many skills are learned out there beyond what is required to be taught to children--beyond what's in the curriculum."

Social Emotional Benefits

Stories shared by all interviewees confirmed that the outdoor classroom is a supportive environment for learners with diverse needs and dispositions. "The forest is a time they can get away from the [behavioral] challenges they face in the classroom," reported one teacher, and the other observed that

> *Getting to see children in a different light, for us is huge. We've got lots more space, no walls, and all those expectations that we have in school are different. We let them take more risks, we say, 'Yes! Climb that tree, go for it!' They get to be themselves, and we get to see the whole child. Every day we go out there [my co-teacher and I] say to each other, 'I never would have seen that side of him if we were inside all the time.'*

These benefits were clear to one grateful parent:

> *We have some behavioral problems with my daughter at school, but because she's free to make her own choices when they're in the woods and not pigeonholed into the classroom, we know it's going to go well. ...I think it's that she knows that today she's not going to get in trouble, she knows she's not going to get sent out of the room where 'bad' kids go, she knows that she can thrive at school at least one day a week.*

The outdoor classroom can offer ways to thrive for all students. One parent volunteer noted that even her own daughter who "does not struggle with managing her body and her behavior" found other ways to grow on Wednesdays. "She's shy and slow to join in so it toughened her up and made her more willing to roll with the punches. She's more flexible now, I'd say."

Affinity for an Active Lifestyle

Increased opportunity to play and learn outdoors, whatever the weather, seems to be having some lifestyle benefits as well for the Hartland students. Two parents shared stories of the impacts on their children:

> *I was concerned about this program because my daughter had zero interest in nature when the school year was starting. But we're Vermonters so all we have is the outdoors, so to have a kid who didn't want to go outdoors was a bummer. But now she will look at us and*

she'll say, 'Let's go on a nature walk!' And I'm thinking, 'What did you do with my child?' This happened within the first four Wednesdays! That has been awesome for our family because we thought we just had an 'indoor kid'.

On the weekends we'd say, 'Let's go for a hike' and in the past she would be resistant and would make one of us carry her. This toughened her up, made her much more willing to be outdoors, and outdoors for longer periods of time. That was an effect I saw right away. Through the program she saw that being outdoors wasn't just hiking. It introduced her to all these ways that she could be herself in the outdoors.

Before this she was into nail polish and 'What are you going to do for me?' and now she's out there building fairy houses and coming home with science skills and rocks in her pockets.

Sowing seeds

These benefits have not gone unnoticed by the rest of the Hartland faculty. All grade levels, K-8, have visited the outdoor classroom, with 1st through 3rd grades visiting almost weekly for shorter periods. Some of these early adopters have already created a second outdoor classroom space far enough from the first to preserve the magical isolation of the kindergarteners' woodland home. The first grade team intends to expand their outdoor time to a full day in the coming school year.

The building administrator expressed great support for future expansion of the program:

You could see all grades benefiting from it. You can try to drum stuff into their heads five days a week and they probably only get three days of it at best. So that day outdoors is probably going to make them listen better on the other four days indoors. And there are a lot of things you can do to make their learning real out there...the only thing that holds you back is your imagination.

The program's appeal has not been lost on the broader community. One parent mentioned that friends who have children attending other schools are "jealous of what we have," and another noted that recently she had "heard of families who factored this program into their decision to move to Hartland."

Bending Toward the Sun

Back in their classroom towards the end of the day, children are writing and drawing in their science journals. Not surprisingly, one boy is busy writing about the animal tracks he followed, another child is drawing the biggest, bluest sky one can imagine, and several students are proudly documenting the very first moments of their day, hours earlier--the "big, big hill" they made it down safely, together.

Hartland Elementary School's Wednesday in the Woods Routine

- Children assemble in the classroom, pack up small matching backpacks with lunch and water bottles, and dress in layers for the weather.
- Enter the woods across the playing fields, and pause for "Tree Stop" at the woods' edge. At this giant, fallen tree at the top of the hill leading down to their outdoor classroom, kids sit, take in the view, sing a woods song, and discuss the day's plan.
- Steep descent to the site, holding onto a rope tied tree to tree, or tumbling on ahead.
- Gather briefly around the fire pit.
- Children and adults head to their sit spot for quiet observations, then small groups gather with an adult to share what they noticed, changes they observed.
- Gather around the fire for snack.
- Choice time (belly sliding, wandering, building forts, tracking animals, gazing at the sky, making nature collections.
- Offerings: kids have 3-4 choices offered by attending adults. Sometimes they are assigned to a group, usually they choose their preferred place.
- Lunch around the fire circle.
- Back in the classroom: writing and drawing in journals, blogging about time outdoors (See the class blog at http://wednesdayinthewoods.blogspot.com/)

Case Study: Ludlow Elementary School

Many people know Ludlow, a town of about 2000 in south central Vermont, as the home of Okemo Mountain ski resort. There's a smaller (both in number and stature) group of people who know it as the home of Dirt City. "Discovered" by a pair of local kindergarteners, the main attraction at Dirt City is not a ski hill, but a giant pine tree, whose tipped-up root ball stands 10-12 feet high, with a gully and a trickle of water running beneath. Every Friday, the townspeople of Dirt City, Ludlow's kindergarten and first graders, spend the school day running along the length of that downed pine tree, dodging in and out of the branches, spotting woodland neighbors, all the while solving problems together, reading and writing, and learning the difference between a risk and a hazard. According one of their teachers,

> *They really believe Forest Friday is their world, and their classroom. I try to make the [indoor] classroom theirs, but in their mind it's still mine, not theirs. They join me in the classroom, but out there, in Dirt City, they have ownership. They find these places and they name these places.*

These young Vermonters are taking part in an emerging wave of Forest Days programs cropping up across Vermont and New Hampshire. While playing and learning in the woods is still a novel concept in today's schools, in Vermont it is a time honored tradition almost as old as the hills themselves.

Something Old, Something New

Located right on Main Street near the heart of town, Ludlow Elementary School serves preK-6th grade and enrolls about 140 students. Ludlow's kindergarten teacher, a classroom veteran with over three decades at the school and nearing retirement, was beginning to feel dissatisfied with the direction of K-1 instructional

Case Study Data Sources: Ludlow Elementary School
- 2 Classroom teachers, formal interviews
- (2 classroom teachers also participated in a one hour focus group on the topic of Forest Days programs)
- 1 Principal, formal interview
- 1 Reading specialist, formal interview
- 3 Parents (one a school board member), formal interviews
- Review of slides, classroom blog

approaches. "I never thought as a kindergarten teacher I'd be sitting behind an instructional table for a large part of my day. It's not how I used to teach," she reflected.

She was also noticing the effects of this more sedentary approach on her students. In the winter, she'd have to teach some of the kids how to go sledding--something one might consider the birthright of a Vermont child. The trouble with this, she noted, is not just that exercise and fresh air are good for human bodies but that "our kids aren't even learning basic things like how to keep themselves safe, to make good judgements, cause and effect. Being outdoors is when kids learn that."

Ludlow Elementary's principal offered a similar concern observing that "Thirty years ago kids played outside, and then because of the way society is, and how scared for safety we've become, now a kid can't problem solve anything without a parent or adult intervening."

The kindergarten and first grade teachers were ready to reclaim what they saw being lost. They attended a statewide kindergarten conference whose theme was outdoor education, and came away inspired, alert to new possibilities for their classrooms. "We wanted to see how we could give students a more developmentally appropriate kindergarten and first grade, and still meet the academic demands," reported the kindergarten teacher.

Just behind the school, tucked in between some dead-end residential roads, lay a small parcel of woods. In it were the remnants of a long abandoned high school ropes course, just enough development to spark a vision. The next steps came naturally for the teaching team, and, supported wholeheartedly by their principal, the school board, and the parent community, they launched Forest Fridays in the fall of 2016. Teachers, students, and volunteers worked together to develop a space that included benches around a fire circle, a small shelter, and an appropriate place to go when you are already in nature but nature is still calling.

> "The music teacher brought her guitar up in the woods and they're singing and dancing and playing. This is what childhood is all about."
> -Parent of first grader

This is the destination once a week on Forest Fridays. The kindergarten and first grade teachers take both their classes out--about 30 students--with a dedicated parent volunteer, and are joined weekly by a combination of enthusiastic literacy, music, art, and P.E. specialists who weave their disciplines into the day's activities.

Stepping Back

The multitude of benefits students receive from this weekly, day-long opportunity to own and be immersed in the natural world beyond Ludlow Elementary's buildings was clear in interviews with Ludlow teachers, parents, a school board member, and an administrator. A vital theme that echoed across all of these groups was the benefits that come with teaching children to evaluate the difference between risks and hazards, and stepping back to let them manage their own behavior. The kindergarten teacher said,

We see minimal conflict in the forest. We try to model solving your own problems, and we focus on how to negotiate, how to do a self-evaluation. We teach them about the difference between a safety hazard and a risk, and frankly this all happens with minimal prompting in the forest.

According to the principal, the strategy used by the teachers and chaperones is this: the adults are all tuned in, but their approach is hands-off. "They let them really try, take a risk, maybe not succeed the first time, try again. It's really about building up perseverance," she said.

Allowing students to take risks, devise their own experiments, and learn to solve problems independently means giving them more opportunities to make choices and plot their own activities. But with five and six year olds, this must be balanced with some structure and boundaries. Striving to strike a balance between structure and choice, teachers plan activity stations throughout the woods--tracking, math games, plant anatomy drawings, or hiking, for instance--and students are then free to choose where to go. If there are three stations, they will be available for three weeks, and students have the option of going deeply into the one choice all three weeks, or sampling each

offering. The teachers explain that they are trusting the children to follow their own best learning paths.

By all accounts, the teachers' trust in their students was not misplaced. As one parent reported, "My daughter would never have tried dough on a stick if I had offered it at home. And now she loves it, and she climbs trees, and she's not afraid to get dirty. She's blossoming out there." Another parent noted that her daughter had lacked confidence, but being in the woods on Fridays has given her a chance to test herself and try new things, and to grow more confident in the process. Children are trying out new athletic activities like snowshoeing, identifying animal scat by shape and color rather than saying "oh, gross" and, related one parent, "kids who are used to gatorade and soda are trying wild edible concoctions and herbal tea over the fire--and they're asking for seconds."

> *"I think the kids are learning how to play again. They're learning how to cooperate without us managing it, without us plotting it all out for them. It automatically happens. Kids group themselves up, they get to choose what to do, they figure out how they're going to play cooperatively."*
> -Principal

Digging In

Forest Fridays is not just about the freedom of playing in the woods. The parents, teachers, and administrators who were interviewed about Forest Days offered a collection of stories, that taken together, paint a picture of deep student engagement in their learning, which has been linked to various important academic outcomes. One research-based approach to understanding school engagement defines three forms of engagement: behavioral, cognitive, and emotional. The stories that follow illustrate how Forest Fridays provide a rich environment for Ludlow's students to fully engage.

Behavioral engagement

Behavioral engagement includes following rules, refraining from disruptive behavior, and constructive participation in class activities. A parent who is also a licensed mental health counselor said she notices fewer behavior problems out in the woods.

> It's so much more hands on, and the difference helps tremendously for kids who have attention problems. There is more of a collaboration on what feels safe, and you're putting it on them to determine if they feel like they're in control. It teaches them to feel out the difference between what's safe or not, instead of dictating that.

The principal echoed this observation, "I watch how active so many of these students are in a classroom, and I see how much time teachers spend working on management issues in a classroom. But up in a forest those behavior issues seem to disappear. It's amazing."

The first grade teacher shared the story of a student who "struggles behaviorally in the classroom," but after a few experiences of problem solving around behavior issues in the forest,

> We saw this shift in him where he was more engaged and more aware of himself, and academically he then took on this theme of being a learner. We think it has had an impact on him. Whether it was the forest days, his own growing maturity, or the combination of the two, we've seen a real difference in that boy.

Cognitive Engagement

Children are cognitively engaged when they are invested in their learning and putting focused intellectual effort into mastering tasks. Ludlow's principal perfectly describes how this manifests at Forest Days:

Their level of focus and concentration improves given a greater level of choice and motivation. One little girl comes to mind. For her to sit still in the classroom for three minutes is nearly impossible, but up in the forest when they go to their chosen Sit Spot to do their 10 minute, quiet observation, well it's amazing. There she is, doing it. After Sit Spot they come back to talk about what they've noticed, what has been changing over time and seasons. Their observation skills exceed my 3rd, 4th, 5th graders by far. It's incredible to hear them.

Core academic subjects benefit as well. The Title One reading teacher leads a literacy activity in the outdoor classroom each week inviting students to dramatize stories to encourage greater reading comprehension. After a story about boats, the students built a snow canoe, hopped in and acted out the characters and plot line of the story as he re-read the tale. In these reenactments the children often memorize lines from the story, each child speaking their lines for an audience as they act out that portion of the story. A teacher for 35 years, he marveled,

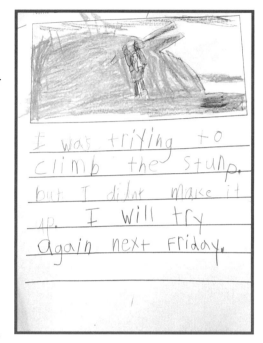

> I've never had kids accelerate so quickly out of my program. We're talking about a small data set here so you'd have to have more years to make this claim, but right now, our reading scores are as high or higher than in past years as of testing in [this same month]. That's all I can say. And as far as their writing it's had a huge impact, whether they're writing about what they're going to do for the day, what they observed, they're excited about it so they're willing to write about it.

A parent of a first grader provided her child's perspective on this:

> We were having issues with reading and speech at the beginning of the year but her reading teacher actually goes up into the woods and he's up there and she sees him up there. So it's more of a community based thing. At first she felt like, 'I have to get reading help, I'm not smart,' so now, guess what, he's up there too and they meet and read in the woods. He recently said, 'I don't think I have to see her anymore because she's above the standard now.' Going in the forest all day is not holding her back, it's only helping.

Emotional engagement

How a child feels about school, teachers, their academic work, and ultimately how much they feel they belong are all aspects of emotional engagement. The kindergarten teacher articulated how the children's enthusiasm for Fridays motivates their school attendance and boosts their confidence.

> I have kids who have been sick Monday through Thursday but they made it for Friday. And for my kindergarteners who are challenged most by academic pressures, they'll come in on Wednesday and they say "Is it Forest Friday yet? We've been waiting so long!

One boy whom she described as "low functioning" resists his writing assignments throughout the week. But on Friday morning the children are required to write their "forest plan" before they can head to the woods, and on that morning, she says, "he is so genuinely motivated. I can read

everything he is communicating! There is a lot of fear for him otherwise. On forest day there is no fear, he is so motivated to get his plan down and get outside."

Engaging others

Among such programs, Ludlow's is notable for including first graders too. Beyond these two classes, some of the approach of Forest Days in letting students evaluate and manage their behavior is beginning to spread throughout the school. A teacher related,

> Sticks were never allowed on the playground, adults were running around saying, 'Don't pick that up, put that down,' all through recess. Then the principal spent a day in the forest and then she went on the playground and she's watching the kids play, digging on the hillside, digging in the rocks, and she said, 'Well, hmm, that's very natural kids' play.' But before that it was banned. Now kids are able to carry sticks around on the playground. I haven't heard people running around telling them not to. So that's shifting, kids have been able to play with stones, pick up sticks, they're able to pick up snow and not be told to put it down.

Forest Fridays have been a topic at staff meeting and the entire staff visited the site on an inservice day. According to the kindergarten teacher, the school staff in general is beginning to take more of a "See if you can figure that out" approach to managing the students at recess. Beyond the free play time of recess, teacher of older grades are now starting to figure out how they can integrate the outdoor classroom into their students' studies.

Parents noted that their children are leading them into new types of exploration at home. A first grader's mother happily reported that she had to dust off her old snowshoes because her daughter had become so motivated to get out on the trails in winter.

> Because of [my daughter's] new skill at snowshoeing, we started snowshoeing as a family. I hadn't gone out in years! But out on the trail she'll point out tracks, notice scat, and then she'll figure out what animal it is. She's motivating us and she's teaching the family too.

The buzz about Forest Fridays has drawn strong support from all across the school community. The literacy specialist remarked, "The number of parent volunteers is incredible.... [The teachers] are having to even turn away parents. It's thrilling." Teachers' husbands have been volunteering, local firemen came to instruct the children about fire safety, and even the school janitor (a maple sugar producer) is getting involved in the teaching. "Everyone heard about it and came to the door saying, 'How can we help, how can we be part of it?'," said the kindergarten teacher.

Local business has gotten involved as well. The students are always prepared for any weather thanks to a grant from Okemo Mountain ski resort that covered the cost of winter coats, snowpants, and rain suits.

Looking to the Future

Asked whether all these benefits come with some drawbacks, such as missed instructional time, the Ludlow principal replied confidently,

> From my observation, they're getting more than what they're getting in the classroom. The math that they do out there--whether it's temperature, or measuring the height of the snow or a tree or adding this to that--and the reading, writing, science--it's off the charts. And in social studies the sense of community and responsibility and democracy--all of that is being met and then some. And the thing is, it sticks. It's happening in a very real life situation for those kids. I could ask a kid, 'What did you do four weeks ago up at Forest Friday?' and they can tell me word for word. It absolutely sticks.

Reflecting on where they had come from and where they were going the principal said, "I'm glad we're able to do this. It will be something that will continue at Ludlow Elementary School for a very long time whether it's these teachers or other teachers."

Meanwhile, back in Dirt City, the kids seem to know just what to do all on their own.

Ludlow Elementary School's Forest Friday "Typical Day"
- First grade and kindergarten work in their classrooms making forest plans and preparing for the day outdoors.
- Walk together to the forest. Set up the site with a fire, portable bathroom, table for s'mores.
- Morning Meeting: All students sit together on logs around fire. Greetings, temperature check, review activities.
- Children move to their adopted Sit Spots for sensory observations, spending six minutes on their own, six minutes sharing observations with a small group.
- Snack time around the fire. Teacher shares home baked muffins.
- Children revolve through station activities, which might include a math activity, scientific drawings, plant identification, hiking and trail planning.
- Free Play for nearly an hour.
- Specials teachers join the group outdoors and students do PE and Music activities. (One adult returns to the school to bring lunches back out for students.)
- Lunch in the forest and more Free Play.
- Pack up/Clean up the outdoor classroom and head down the trail.
- Back in the classroom, it's time to undress, check for ticks, wash hands.
- For the last hour of the day, indoors, students may identify plants observed in the forest, read nature books, or work on writing blog posts.
- Closing circle as a K-1 team.

Case Study: Mount Lebanon Elementary School

For one of the three kindergarten classes at Mount Lebanon Elementary School, Wednesdays are no ordinary day. There are otter slides, acorn families, and full bodied physics experiments to invent, and there are 16 pairs of insulated mud boots lined up and ready to assist in the action. Attendance is higher on Wednesdays, and the young students' spirits match. The kindergarten teacher notes that their enthusiasm for writing soars, their drawings contain more details, and their organizational skills are honed.

What is the secret of Wednesdays for West Lebanon, New Hampshire kindergarteners? It's Wednesday in the Woods, a day when the children head for the wooded hill behind their school, eyes bright, thinking caps on, parent and teacher chaperones in tow, to spend the morning--rain and snow, mud and sun--learning with trees, fire, gravity, and birdsongs as their classroom.

Hatching the Plan

A site for a forest kindergarten wasn't immediately obvious to the Mount Lebanon principal, though she had a strong hunch that this was the ticket for some of her youngest charges. Located just a mile or so up the street from a busy regional shopping hub in West Lebanon, New Hampshire, the elementary school is surrounded by a handful of three-story apartment complexes in a squarely suburban neighborhood. A relatively small wooded area behind the school stretches up a sudden, steep hill just beyond the playground. One day, on a whim, the principal scaled the tree covered hill and, to her surprise and delight, discovered a 'shelf' of flat land nestled in the woods, just out of sight from the surrounding built world. From there, she knew it was possible. She and an enthusiastic kindergarten teacher visited several other schools' Forest Day classrooms, received the blessing of the superintendent, confirmed insurance coverage, and--since gathering for meals, warming, and storytelling around a fire circle is central for many Forest Days programs--received a fire permit from the fire department.

Case Study Data Sources: Mount Lebanon Elementary School
- 1 classroom teacher, formal interview
- (classroom teacher also participated in a one hour focus group on the topic of Forest Days programs)
- 1 principal, formal interview
- 1 classroom aids, formal interview
- 1 English Language Learners teacher, formal interview
- 2 parents, in person and by phone
- Students, informal conversations
- Onsite observation of outdoor classroom and class, not during field day
- Review of classroom blog

From a generation of teachers who had since retired, the principal learned that there had been a time when more Mount Lebanon children played in those woods, and trails had criss-crossed the wooded hillside. The paths were overgrown from lack of use, so--tapping into yet another generation--she contacted an Eagle Scout, a former Mount Lebanon Elementary school

student. "With great enthusiasm and sense of purpose," said the principal, the young man revived the trails of the past, cleared hazardous branches, and cut stumps to create the fire circle.

Each week, teachers bring a portable fire pit and pop up latrine tent and pail up to the site--both features are temporary in the hopes of deterring weekend parties at the spot--and the kindergarteners head out, accompanied by their teacher, a classroom aide, and often by a parent volunteer, a special educator, and an English Language Learning specialist. Unlike some Forest Days programs, they spend the morning rather than the full day, opting to come in for the nutritious school lunch provided free to many children in the population.

Place-based education, an educational pedagogy with which Forest Days programs align, promotes the use not only of natural environments but of local built communities as a means to ground learning in children's tangible world. The prospect of using the wooded hillside as a classroom prompted a dive into the human local community as well--the kindergarten teacher described a shining example of emergent place-based social studies and science curriculum that unfolded in preparation Wednesdays in the Woods:

Since all the kids don't have the outdoor gear they needed, we got a grant to buy boots. We walked down to West Leb Feed and Supply, explored the neighborhood, learned about the business, kids tried on boots, we talked about the different weights of feed. We then wrote thank you notes to the store owners, and even when we mailed the letters, it was a chance to get to know our neighborhood, walking to the mailbox down the road. The Feed and Supply were so impressed they then came out to our classroom to do lessons about what local birds live here and how to create a bird feeder. Kids learned about bird calls and now they listen for them when when we're up in the woods. The grandparents of one of my students then came in and did a lesson on different birds. All of these lessons expanded out from going to the get the boots!

Taking Flight

The outdoors opens up new opportunities for developmentally appropriate growth in three key areas noted by the nationwide, early childhood nature immersion program, Tinkergarten. According to Tinkergarten's program theory, students will demonstrate seven key cognitive capacities (curiosity; creativity; problem solving; persistence/grit; focus/self control; imagination; naturalist); five social capacities (communication; empathy; collaboration; self

regulation; self reliance); and a handful of physical capacities including sensory awareness; gross and fine motor skills, and the skills to embody an active lifestyle.

Interviews conducted with Mount Lebanon parents, teachers, and an administrator elicited compelling examples of all of these qualities. The principal captured the multitude of benefits for students in this way, "There's more to learning than just sitting and learning in an academic setting outside you're learning about your body, balance and safety and exploration, taking chances, and the richness of learning about our fauna and flora out there."

Cognitive Capacities: Science, Math, and Literacy in Action

Being outdoors creates unexpected, engaging opportunities. Slopes and snow, for instance, provide a canvas for testing physics concepts such as force, friction, and gravity. The principal described a Wednesday visit with the group:

We were using words like 'momentum' as they were sliding on the hill. And then they were rolling these big snowballs and comparing their speed. There was this physics learning going on in the moment. Those kinds of opportunities pop up that you wouldn't necessarily plan for.

Interviewees pointed to a host of examples of children constructing their own learning while playing, and of adults capitalizing on this opportunity by modeling play and problem solving, interspersing key activities, and offering vocabulary words to enhance understanding.

One father deeply appreciated the hands-on, tactile nature of the learning process on Wednesdays, noting that his son seems to be "put off from traditional academics." He expressed delight at seeing his son experiencing "academic success" engaging directly in the living world while designing a teeter totter from logs or tracking a deer.

> *"I want him to like school and build that habit and expectation of 'I'm going to school because I like it!' Not, 'I'm going to school and they're going to force me to sit at a desk all day.' Having this opportunity to just go out and be five is huge for my son."*
> *-Kindergarten parent*

Exposure to real world experiences can fuel energy and interest for writing and reading activities as well. The kindergarten teacher noted that students practice their letters and numbers using sticks and natural objects on the forest floor, and they refer back to photographs of these in the classroom when practicing writing. She also

selects early reading books that tie directly to their observations outside. Recently, the students spotted a deer in the woods, having learned to identify the animal's scat and tracks. After this captivating experience, reported the teacher, "I was able to find one of those early steps toward reading books that was about a deer right after we had actually seen a deer. They got so excited about reading that book!"

The English Language Learners (ELL) teacher concurred with the classroom teacher's observation that the students' writing, too, seemed to be richer and more detailed when they were reflecting on their outdoor days, adding, "To be a good writer you have to have first hand exposure, so when they come in after the day in the woods, they know exactly what they touched and felt and experienced."

Prior to launching Wednesdays in the Woods at Mount Lebanon, other principals had assured the Mount Lebanon administrator that "kids are academically right in stride with their peers." A parent of a current kindergartener echoed this sentiment, noting she had no concern about her son's readiness for first grade. She responded with confidence that he would be "right on par or more ready. I think a greater variety of experiences can only help you in tackling a new grade and subject matter."

Social Capacities: Developing Social Emotional Competence

All interviewees referred to the social, psychological, behavioral, and emotional benefits they see in outdoor days for students. A classroom aide described one child's experience: "This one boy is quiet in class but when we're out in the woods setting he is animated and running. He says, 'Do you want to come see my hideout?' He engages more with people, he's more outgoing, he seems more comfortable." Indeed, when Mount Lebanon faculty went to visit other examples of Forest Days programs, a few teachers challenged them to identify the students who are designated to receive one-to-one attention from an aide. The principal said, "Those kids don't need one on one support when they're out in the woods. They know how to manage themselves, they're busy, they're active, they're not needing as much redirection. Philosophically it didn't surprise me, and to actually see it it was really beautiful."

Giving children the opportunity to exercise their imagination and define their activities, according to their teacher, seems to engender a feeling of empowerment:

> Having that exposure every day each week to be free in the outdoors, it's sort of like a power for them. They're in control of what they're doing. In the classroom, everything is for a

purpose. On Wednesdays, they have a chance to be in control of what they use--they get to tell a stick what it is.

Faculty and parents shared stories, for instance, of captains at the helm of their own log "boat", families of adventurous acorns, and fishermen "fishing" off a log.

And the ELL teacher noticed that she sees fewer conflicts between children: "Everybody owns the woods. They don't see that things out there are owned by anyone, so the sharing conflicts don't come up out there. That attitude seems to translate back into the classroom."

Physical Capacities: Bodies in Motion

For their part, kindergarteners described their favorite Wednesday activities as "making tunnels" and "building stuff" and "playing Sharks on the Dock, a game I made up." In an age of increasing concern about childhood obesity and inactivity, the children seem to know intuitively know how to make the most of this environment. "All of the students knew what to do the minute the got outside--no one saying, "I'm bored, what should i do?" There were no little girls standing around not wanting to get dirty. I could see that outdoor days were not gender based at all." The children are constantly in motion, using their bodies to climb trees, and ascend and descend the big hills, noted the principal, learning about balance in the process:

> *The other day they were sliding down the path on their backs, the kids who got some speed going the were holding their bodies in a different kind of balance, on the right place on the back. You watch the others watching that, and figuring out how to hold their bodies to they too can go faster. Then they're balancing on logs. Hiking up there in and of itself, it's on a big slope so they're using their arms and hands and bodies to climb around up there, I see them using their bodies in a gross motor way that has to be good for them...I see them getting more coordinated.*

Enthusiasm for School

Attention to the development of all of these cognitive, social, and physical capacities on Wednesdays at Mount Lebanon seems to go hand in hand with a growing enthusiasm for school. The teacher noted,

> *The most significant benefit to kids I've seen has been their enjoyment of school -- enjoyment of school in it's purest form. When we're up there they show just total joy at being outside. Even in the trickiness of a cold or wet day, they are overwhelmingly asking to go outside. When we have choice time, kids ask, can we go outside instead? If it's motivating kids to come to school, to enjoy being in school, that's huge. And also school as a place--a place of learning but also a place that's part of a neighborhood, and part of the natural world.*

A father related the common story of asking his children, "What did you do today at school?" and getting the reply "Nothing." But, he said, on Wednesdays, it's always an enthusiastic sharing of the day's doings. He values a newsletter that comes home with pictures and stories of the

day, and says his son "circles his picture, tells about what they're doing, reminds him to do a tick check. He's always really proud to tell me what he did that day."

The story of a little boy who was reluctant to make the transition to kindergarten weaves together the benefits--academic, social, physical, and enthusiasm for school--described here by the kindergarten teacher:

> One boy who was frequently absent, and hadn't gone to preschool, didn't want to come to school most days, but always comes on Wednesdays. He has this ongoing fort building project. It's the center of what he does every week--he uses certain materials, and he has set it up with his friends so everyone is clear that this space is ongoing.
> By contrast, one of the rules on the playground is that forts can't stay. If there's a fort up, anyone is allowed to take it down. In the forest, we allow the ownership--that's how deeper play is--he's allowed to keep going back to this one thing that he really, really loves. He rarely writes or draws about anything else--his drawings are about what happened with his fort each week.

The freedom to construct (and invest in) his own play scenarios, freely in the woods, allowed him to build confidence with other children, developing social connections and self confidence. It allowed him to invest in something that gave him focus, that challenged his abilities in designing, building,

> "Sometimes I think there's too much testing. You're so interested in finding out where they are, you take away what they are really interested in."
> -Classroom aide

problem solving, and--ultimately--creative expression through writing and drawing. In turn, this focus and confidence has meant that, while he often resists going to school, "He has never missed a Wednesday."

The cultivation of this sort of enthusiasm is no light matter, as showing up and being engaged are simple yet meaningful precursors to success in all aspects of ones of life.

Soaring Beyond this Schoolyard

While the school's administrator does not envision the outdoor classroom becoming a whole school endeavor, she enjoys seeing other classes head up the hill occasionally for read aloud or other brief encounters. As interest and enthusiasm grows, she notes that other teachers may use the resource more, and has attended to the program's sustainability by building the cost of outfitting students into the budget. Her vision, however, spans beyond the slope behind her school. "People call me up and ask about it, and I have as many hours as it takes to support anyone who's interested in this," she said.

Given their success this first year of Wednesday in the Woods, even with limited natural surroundings, she encourages other principals to be catalysts in their schools. She couples the abundance of screens in students' lives and the dangers--perceived and real--that some kids encounter in their neighborhoods, both of which keep them indoors, and contrasts that with the "overwhelming bank of research elaborating the importance of time outdoors. It's the perfect time to start something like this." Much like the momentum students studied as snowballs raced down the big slope, she sees perfect momentum for the spread of Forest Days:

> There is so much evidence that justifies this kind of thing in a school. If you can't see it with your own eyes, there's actually data and evidence. It's really great time from a leadership perspective to step forward in a bold way and do something different in public education.

And, as Mount Lebanon has shown, one never knows what sites lie all around our schools waiting to be rediscovered by pioneering educators, history-minded community members, and exploring kindergarteners.

Mount Lebanon Elementary's Wednesday in the Woods Routine

- Morning jobs in the classroom, including a Forest Day plan.
- As a class, determine what gear needs to be worn and whether we are eating in the classroom or the Woods.
- Call the Fire Department for a burn permit.
- Hike up to our space with an adult in the front and back of the line.
- Greetings around the fire circle and sharing nature observations. Sharing adult plans (e.g. building words with sticks, looking for tracks, baking bread on sticks) and student plans (e.g. forts building, stream play, making up games).
- Gather back at the fire circle to share stories of the day and sing the Forest Song: "Hasta Luego, Hasta Luego/ Y Adios, Y adios/Nos Gusta el Bosque, Nos Gusta el Bosque/ciao, ciao, ciao."
- Hike down the trail and get cleaned up to be inside.
- Back in the classroom: writing and drawing in story journals, creating class newsletter (See the newsletter at https://sites.google.com/a/sau88.net/mls_cjoanis/announcements)

Cross Cutting Findings

Forest Days Case Studies: A Cross Site View

Hartland Elementary School, Mount Lebanon Elementary School, and Ludlow Elementary Schools are three of about 20 schools in Vermont and New Hampshire where teachers, principals, and supportive community members have mobilized to consistently and deeply integrate learning outdoors into the school week. Dubbed Forest Fridays, Outdoor Mondays, Woods Day, or Wednesday in the Woods, what these programs around the region have in common is one or more teachers who believe that the natural landscape is an appropriate context for learning and that the power of freedom and self-determination will deepen a child's motivation for learning. These programs also have in common a vital support: strong backing from an administrator as well an essential outcome--a lot of happy kids and families.

Each of these schools has created an outdoor learning space that classes can use as a home base during their weekly excursions. There is usually a central gathering circle around a fire pit, sometimes a lean-to in which to keep materials dry, and some form of "bathroom" (perhaps a teepee of sticks for modesty, and a removable bucket). The rest of the classroom is the trees, sky, wildlife, and fresh air in which to move one's body and brain.

The apparent success of the Forest Days programs can be interpreted through a variety of pedagogical and theoretical lenses. Place-based education promotes the use of both natural and built communities as a means to ground learning in children's tangible world, and posits that students will readily engage with what is local, known, and relevant to them. And it is apparent in watching these children and educators in action, that the tenets of Self-Determination Theory (SDT) are at work here: when students experience a sense of competence, autonomy and relatedness, they are more likely to take healthy risks, solve problems creatively, invest in their own learning process, and work cooperatively with others. In short, their motivation for learning flourishes.[3] The rich context for learning (place-based) coupled with the students' experience of the learning environments (self-determined) created conditions for strong engagement with their school experience: cognitively, behaviorally, and emotionally. All of these forms of engagement have been shown to link with success in school.[4]

---

[3] http://www.apa.org/research/action/success.aspx
[4] https://repository.asu.edu/attachments/56844/content/Smith_asu_0010N_10812.pdf

What benefits do we see across sites?

- **Mastery of academic content** *(cognitive engagement)*. Despite a reduction in traditional classroom-based instructional time, all sites reported acceleration of students' reading and writing, science and math skills. Writing was fueled by authentic experiences, and opportunities for real world science projects were abundant. Interviewees reported seeing children

> *"The kids are absolutely learning at least as fast as in the classroom. I don't consider those Fridays non-learning time in any shape or form."*
> -Reading Specialist

engaged in engineering, design, problem solving, observation skills, storytelling, active listening and public speaking, to name a few.

- **Enhanced student enthusiasm for school** *(emotional engagement)*. A natural extension of students' enhanced engagement in learning, and by an attachment to their place, students at all sites showed evidence of an enhanced enthusiasm for going to school. Examples offered included students at multiple sites proudly bringing visitors on weekends or after school to see their outdoor classroom, students laying out clothes the night before in anticipation of the forest day, and higher attendance rates on forest days.

- **Fewer discipline or behavior issues** *(behavioral engagement)*. Perhaps attributable to students' enjoyment of school, all sites reported that students make far less 'trouble' during forest days. Numerous stories about children who often struggle to behave appropriately

> *"I love seeing the deep engagement up there and realizing their capacity for that and realizing that if they can do it out there they can do it in here."*
> -Kindergarten teacher

in the classroom setting, but who were thriving on forest days. One specials teacher noted, "Behavior management issues when we're out there? None, absolutely none. In fact, those kids who have trouble focusing in the classroom, they're different children out there, they're more engaged."

- **Strong community support and participation.** The programs shared enthusiastic support from diverse stakeholders ranging from students' parents to teachers' spouses volunteering weekly at the forest sites; from the music teacher playing guitar in the woods to the custodian teaching maple sugaring; from weekend work parties to donated or discounted clothing and equipment from the community and local businesses.

- **Teamwork and problem solving skills.** Given the space and time to enact one's own agenda, and the raw materials of nature rather than the built structures and fixed-use materials of a playground or classroom, children were reportedly thinking creatively and communicating directly with one another--working cooperatively to create the world they wanted to inhabit for that time.

- **Improved social connectivity for students and teachers**. Teachers and parents across sites reported that students seemed to have more mobility in their friendships on forest days, and that even teachers' own connections with students were enhanced as the traditionally hierarchical classroom structure was replaced by a more collaborative and student-led learning environment.

- **Healthy physical development.** Students built stamina, muscle tone, and gross motor skills as they navigated steep slopes and icy passages; sustained outdoor play for hours a day; and developed the appetite and skills needed to engage themselves and their families in new outdoor activities like snowshoeing or birdwatching.

- **Spread of implementation.** In some cases, teachers from other grade levels planned to start using the outdoor classroom. In other cases, the more hands-off approach to student management was spreading to the playground as the adults began to find that students could take safe risks and make appropriate decisions on their own.

What makes these programs work?

A host of "key ingredients" surfaced as factors that allowed for the smooth creation and sustained success of these Forest Days programs.

- **A spark and a flame.** The spark may come from a teacher attending a conference, reading a book, or having a friend at an existing forest days school; the sustained flame comes from a supportive administrator and school board backing a teacher's efforts. As one teacher said, "We're very fortunate to have a principal who loves to see us doing things from the bottom up."

- **An enthusiastic co-teacher.** While one site had just one teacher running the forest day program, the companionship of a teacher team seemed important. In one case, a new kindergarten teacher position was available and candidates' interest in launching this effort factored heavily into the hiring process. In two cases, the teachers were so inspired by the benefits they saw in joining their classes of children together they began also collaborating on other aspects of their curriculum.

- **Teachers having an affinity group.** All teachers noted how helpful it was to be part of an affinity group--in this case the Outdoor Play and Learning Professional Learning Community[5]--while launching and working out the kinks of this program. Through this

---

[5] This PLC was led by educators Eliza Minnucci and Meg Teachout, with support from the Wellborn Ecology Fund.

Forest Days Case Studies: Hartland, Ludlow, Mount Lebanon, & Cross Cutting Findings

network, they were able to visit outdoor classrooms around the region and swap curriculum ideas with other educators.

- **Establishing boundaries and then trusting kids.** The greater physical freedom of the outdoors allows active kids to thrive in their bodies, and reserved kids to push themselves out of their comfort zones and test limits. "We step back, we keep a watchful eye, but we let them take a little risk and see what happens, and go from there," explained a kindergarten teacher. Parents appreciated this day where their children have "more ability to explore, make mistakes, and problem solve. It's more open, not so regimented."

> "We're trying to just trust them and let them choose. I think in general [society is] micromanaging kids too much."
> -Kindergarten teacher

- **Modeling play and curiosity for students.** Noting that children today are often quite scheduled in their activities, teachers across sites try to model playful activities when children seem at a loss, especially at the beginning of the school year. These teachers, rather than instructing in what to do, engage right into the play, becoming a wild animal, building a snow rabbit, inhabiting a fairy kingdom, creating letters out of sticks on the ground, sliding down a hill, collecting natural objects, lying down in the snow and sky gazing.

- **Maintaining a flexible agenda and attitude.** Whether because of weather conditions, unexpected curiosities in nature, or the whims of children, teachers have struck a balance of mapping out a loose structure for the day and "letting our day mold itself." This flexibility is also about being "playful in our academics." Kindergarten teachers talked about "bringing indoor learning outdoors," flexibly taking advantage of teachable moments.

- **Involving parents and community.** Community assistance is needed in the start-up work of preparing the outdoor classrooms, and there are numerous ongoing roles for volunteers to fill to help keep students safe and engaged. Parents and community members participated in the programs as trail builders, shelter erectors, chaperones, guest leaders, firewood stockers, and many other roles.

What obstacles to implementation (and solutions) did sites encounter?

Asked about challenges faced in implementing this new way of doing things at the three elementary schools, responses were notably few and solutions seemed forthcoming in most cases.

- **Initial skepticism.** Interviewees noted that while several parents and assistant teachers had initially been skeptical about Forest Days, worrying about things such as "my son doesn't like dirt", or wondering about safety and emergency response, no one could think of any real detractors once the programs were up and running. Many shared stories of skeptics won over by the reality of the program in action. Safety issues were addressed in various ways: having the ready support of the social emotional interventionists out in the woods (and back in school if a child needed to stay behind); going out equipped with walkie talkies and phones; regular checks of the natural environment for potential hazards. Clear, consistent communication with parents and the school community regarding the program's purposes and development was noted as a key to success.

- **Staffing wisely.** Choosing support staff (such as paraeducators) who are enthusiastic about the outdoors was important. While very few people mentioned the students having any issues with rain, cold, or other environmental challenges, adults were more likely to balk. Those classroom assistants who had a predisposition to the outdoors were more likely to remain engaged and enthusiastic throughout the year.
- **Keeping students outfitted for all weather.** At a site where all the equipment had not been procured in advance via donations or grant funds, an occasional challenge was students not owning (or remembering to bring) the proper clothing for the weather. Even at this site, however, donations of warm clothing had been collected for families who had less access to all-weather gear, and extra items were available at school when kids forgot things.
- **Site development and maintenance.** Establishing and maintaining a "classroom" in the woods requires personpower, whether it's building trails and fire circles, constructing benches or shelters, or regular removal of hazards like dangling branches. Every teacher relied on help, both at the outset, and for ongoing maintenance, from community members ranging from boy scouts to local retirees. Every teacher reported spending some time on weekends or during summer to ready the site.
- **Site impact.** Perhaps a more persistent challenge that will likely only grow over time and as interest in these programs grows across grade levels, is the wear and tear on the forest sites. In some cases, these programs turn undisturbed forest into a working landscape, the impact of which can be mediated to some degree by attentive stewardship.

Conclusion

The spread of Forest Days programming is a regional and national phenomenon. Like any educational innovation, scale up will be supported by documentation of implementation, challenges, effective practices, and outcomes. This set of case studies provides insights into the processes being implemented and outcomes emerging at three New England sites. The evidence from these profiles suggests that Forest Days are a promising intervention that not only supports academic learning but offers numerous social, emotional, physical, and community-level benefits to diverse participants. The benefits seem to far outweigh any challenges brought forth, indicating that this pedagogical approach is worthy of consideration by a broader audience.

Proud and patriotic, forest kindergartners and their forest flag.

About the Authors

Eliza Minnucci was raised in Deerfield, New Hampshire. She now makes her home in Tunbridge, Vermont with her husband, Keith and sons, Finn and Auden. Before teaching Kindergarten in Quechee, Vermont, she taught young children in Zihuatanejo, Mexico, Chicago, Seattle, and Fort Yukon, Alaska. She holds a bachelor's degree from the University of Chicago, teacher certification from the Upper Valley Educators Institute and a master's degree in education from New England College. On hiatus from the classroom, she supports teachers in cultivating nature-based play and learning for their students through consultation and teaching the Nature-based Early Childhood Curriculum course at Antioch University New England. She is a frequent presenter at In Bloom conferences throughout New England. She loves snow-rollers, jack-in-the-pulpits and indigo buntings.

*Meghan Teachout (left) and
Eliza Minnucci*

Meghan Teachout was raised in the suburbs of New York City. She has settled in Strafford, Vermont with her husband, Cabot and their three children, Elva, Otto and Ulysses. She received her bachelor's degree from the University of Vermont and completed teacher training at the Upper Valley Educators Institute. With Eliza, she co-founded the Forest Day program at the Ottauquechee School in 2013. She now supports teachers in cultivating nature-based routines by team-teaching, and leading professional learning communities. She loves spring ephemerals, cloud-watching and snowflake shapes.

About Nature-Based Early Childhood Education at Antioch University New England

The Nature-Based Early Childhood Education Certificate (NbEC) program in the Department of Education at Antioch University New England trains teachers, administrators, and founders of nature preschools and forest kindergartens. The nature preschool and forest kindergarten movement has been thriving in Europe for the last thirty years and has taken root in the United States since the beginning of the 21st century. Both nature preschools and forest kindergartens have a uniquely different approach to curriculum than conventional indoor early childhood programs.

The objective of the NbEC program is to make the courses as practical as possible. The goal for each week long or weekend course is to have each student generate a product that is tangibly useful in his/her work situation. This will include program brochures, policy development, business plans, curriculum documentation materials a la Reggio, grant proposals and parent newsletters. Program faculty provide assistance in content and tone so that founders of new programs can be supported in developing materials to launch their programs.

Contact Ellen Doris, NbEC program director, for information or visit the Education Department website at: www.antioch.edu.

Reflections of Forest Day Students

"Forest Days are important because the forest smells good."
"Because it's pretty."
"Because we learn."

"The fallen tree is my favorite place in the forest because
it makes me taller than ever before and I can see the world."

"In the forest I pretend I am a wolf."
"I pretend I am a snowshoe hare."
"I pretend I am a woodsman."
"I like to pretend I am myself."

"On Forest Day I work on the rock pile; I know there is treasure there."
"I work on the construction site; I am the foreman."

"It is good to be out in the cold because it is so quiet."
"If you dress good, you're not cold."

"The good thing about being in the rain is watching the flowers grow."
"It cleans the earth."
"I can't jump in puddles at home."

*– Peter Dargatz's Kindergartners (Sussex, Wisconsin) and
Laura Lewis's Second Graders (Sharon, Vermont)*